ALL IN

Cancer, Near Death, New Life

Caitlin Breedlove

Foreword by adrienne maree brown

PRESS

Advance praise for *All In*:

"In this beautifully written and deeply honest book Caitlin Breedlove brings us on her harrowing journey through cancer. With unflinching emotional, spiritual and political insight, she offers lessons about struggle for us all."
　　　　—**Barbara Smith, author of** *The Truth That Never Hurts*

"Wrestling with what it means to hold death and life in a body with cancer, this is an offering of raw, unfiltered truth of recovery, transmutation, cancer, and life. Her words are a salve for all hearts and medicine for survivors. As well as a blueprint on how to navigate systems of reproductive care when the constellation of queer/trans/femme bodies has been collapsed and forgotten."
　　　　—**Cara Page, author of** *Healing Justice Lineages*

"Required reading for anyone longing to make a wider way for love and justice in the world. Standing in the tradition of our feminist foremothers—think Audre Lorde, think June Jordan—Caitlin allows her particular life-threatening experience to inform a politics already rooted in what it means to show up in one's fullness, no matter the circumstance. I was at once shattered and challenged by the unflinching glimpse she provided of life's fragility and fierceness."
　　　　—**Lisa Anderson, founding director of the Sojourner Truth Leadership Circle**

EMERGENT STRATEGY SERIES

Emergent Strategy by adrienne maree brown
Pleasure Activism by adrienne maree brown
Undrowned by Alexis Pauline Gumbs
We Will Not Cancel Us by adrienne maree brown
Holding Change by adrienne maree brown
Begin the World Over by Kung Li Sun
Fables and Spells by adrienne maree brown
Liberated to the Bone by Susan Raffo
JesusDevil by Alexis De Veaux
Practicing New Worlds by Andrea J. Ritchie
Atoms Never Touch by micha cárdenas

All In: Cancer, Near Death, New Life
Emergent Strategy Series No. 11
© 2024 Caitlin Breedlove
This edition © 2024, AK Press
ISBN: 978-1-84935-530-8
E-ISBN: 978-1-84935-531-5
Library of Congress Control Number: 2023935633

AK Press
370 Ryan Ave. #100
Chico, CA 95973
www.akpress.org
akpress@akpress.org

AK Press
33 Tower St.
Edinburgh EH6 7BN
Scotland
www.akuk.com
ak@akedin.demon.co.uk

The above addresses would be delighted to provide you with the latest AK Press
distribution catalog, which features books, pamphlets, zines, and stylish apparel
published and/or distributed by AK Press. Alternatively, visit our websites for the
complete catalog, latest news, and secure ordering.

Cover design by Herb Thornby
Cover illustration by Ashley Penning, ashleypenning.com

Printed in the USA on acid-free paper

For my ancestors: long and newly dead.

Contents

Foreword
by adrienne maree brown

The first time I read Octavia E. Butler's *Lilith's Brood*, I had not, to my knowledge, lost anyone to cancer. Now, that seems wild and miraculous. Now, I often think of cancer as both a personal and generational enemy, stealing my loved ones from their bodies, exhausting them as they try to live, drowning them in their bodies.

Octavia's Oankaki aliens saw cancer as something generative, of immense genetic value. They wanted to harness its power; they saw it as the contribution humans were making to the universe. I have struggled trying to look through this lens, despite the beauty and rigor of Octavia's reimagining.

From an analytical standpoint, I see cancer as a way the toxins we have unleashed into the world are cycling back in and through us, because we are literal parts of the world we overuse, misuse, and abuse. In *All In*, my comrade Caitlin Breedlove describes her experience as a consequence of life under capitalism, where exploitation—and self-exploitation—is standard operating procedure. "The machine of overwork often convinces us our pain is normal, setting our standards of suffering to autopilot, set to run until we just fall down one day," she writes.

She also calls cancer a disease of overproduction. As Breedlove observes, "overproduce is what [cancer] does.

How do we heal from a disease that does that in a society obsessed with excess and overproduction? Cancer is an inability in the body to decipher between healthy and unhealthy cells. It is a disease that is without boundaries, a system that uncontrollably spawns its deadly and damaging products."

Cancer is also such a clear consequence of nuclear bombs and radiation and pollution and eating plastic and poisoning water, and forgetting to honor the land as we swallow it. And in the same way that the choices that most harm us and the earth are imprecise and fatal, cancer is currently an imprecise and often fatal consequence, generating death in the bodies of humans who have spent their lives loving the earth and fighting the toxins.

From an emergent strategy standpoint, I have been longing for more wisdom directly from the heart of those battling with, dancing with, cancer. And in her memoir, Caitlin describes her frustrating search for authentic narratives about living with cancer, and about finding very little that resonated with her. "Most of the literature that I find feels like it found its way to recognition and audience through experiences, stories, and energies that are nothing at all like what I am going through," she writes. "Much of it feels so saccharine, so positive, pink-ribboned, white, straight, and suburban. It is sugarcoating things that are not and should not taste sweet."

Indeed, we need books that help us understand what is happening from the inside out, and how to be in community, how to hold each other tight as we embody the huge shifts necessary to make a cancerous world part of our collective past, instead of an inevitable future. It is what *is* right now, and for the foreseeable future. To understand it, survive it, and shift our relationship to both cancer *and* our loved ones in cancer's grip, we need texts *from* those surviving cancer *for* others who are touched by it.

Caitlin says she searched for "stories, accounts, and reckonings of this experience from the perspective of outsiders from the dominant story of how this all goes . . . for stories of going through this told by women, queers, people of color, immigrants, poor people, by parents. I find some. Not a lot."

Thankfully, for those of us engaged in the same quest, Caitlin is a trustworthy, vulnerable, and eloquent guide, inviting us to walk with her, suffer with her, grieve with her, and learn with her. "Swimming in seas of all things privatized, numb, and individual, our times make our own shapes more difficult to feel. We're overstimulated but spiritually starving," she writes. "This living from within outward can allow us to push out new bulbs, leaves, and flowerings; and, in doing so, the rotted, the addictive, the stuck matter can be pushed out of us. There is no nobility in how I change; I simply am new growth because the old has run out of space on the branch."

I believe her amazing chronicle is in deep conversation with a sister text, Audre Lorde's *The Cancer Journals*, a lodestar since its publication in 1980. "*The Cancer Journals*," Caitlin writes, "stands alone." Because, as she continues, Lorde is "the only woman writer who lived with cancer I have ever read who wrote with raw truth about what it meant for her body, her sexuality, her mind, her relationships, and her children to suffer like this."

The rarity of such text makes me even more grateful for Caitlin's singular book, a gift that she calls "a science experiment, a faith experiment, a magical alchemical experiment." As an organizer, activist, and thinker, I have known her to be a human of deep questions, thorough research and emotional integrity. When Caitlin received her diagnosis, when she shared it, I could immediately feel how much it meant to her to tell the truth about what she was experiencing. What surprised me, and deeply moved me, was her capacity to make the truth beautiful, even as she told the ugliest parts. Caitlin puts life into each sentence, even as she moves too close to death. Her survival is a miracle, and so is her testimony.

Introduction

The process of illness that brings us near death is often a process of erasure. We lie between life and death, and most people avert their gaze from us. Most of us in this country also avoid dwelling too much on the dead themselves, though they are unfathomably legion and ever-present. They are the water we drink, the land we walk on, the food we eat, the cells we are made of.

We are afraid and yet we are obsessed, scaring ourselves with zombie movies, but the real undead/unalive, those of us who hang in a certain balance, are largely ignored. We elicit pity, guilt, and discomfort. Our stories are told for us, people run marathons on our behalf. The half-dead, the near-dead, the undead: our presence can be frightening. But witches say, where there is fear there is power. There is power in what we fear; there is a power we wield when we are feared. It is a time in the world where these sayings, these stories, and these worldviews must be shared widely again.

I developed ovarian cancer in my late thirties. Ovarian cancer kills the vast majority of its victims; there are few survivors. This is largely because there is limited testing, and it is almost always caught too late. Its symptoms are so generic (bloating, fatigue) that any tired woman would not notice them, and most poor and working-class women would simply endure them. I wrote what you are about to read for an audience of myself and my ancestors. Writing for such an audience is a simple task; it is difficult to believe it took me almost forty years to figure that out. I wrote it also out of a matured vision of the purpose of my social justice work in this lifetime: a sense of contribution over consolation or competition.

This book is not exactly a memoir. It is a chronicle, a science experiment, a faith experiment, a magical alchemical experiment. It marks a tally of days. I hope it is of use to others, but I know it is of great use to me.

In January of 2021, while our world endured the isolation of COVID, I received a quick spiral of diagnoses that resulted in three cancer-related surgeries in less than three months. The winter of 2020 had started with relief: many of us had worked hard (and relatively well) together to defeat Trump. The previous four years of his presidency had brought me back to my organizing spirit and, while my peers and I were overworked and worn out, I felt some measure of calm when he was voted out. Alongside the battles of 2020, a small spirit had been warmly pestering me, like a child asking to be born. She brought me messages, bodily communiqués that doctors call "symptoms." These resulted in a diagnosis of ovarian cancer, the deadliest of all gynecological cancers and one that disproportionately impacts queer women, transmen, Jewish women of Eastern European descent, gender nonconforming people, and older women. It feeds on those who can't go to a doctor and those who convince ourselves we do not need to.

It is a cancer that lives and grows far inside the body. In my case, it came to me after years of terribly painful periods, with days of cramps and heavy bleeding. Continuous travel for work meant I rarely went to a doctor; I told myself that I ate alright and exercised. I had visited a gynecologist a few times, but they had not figured out what was wrong and only suggested birth control pills, which I politely would refuse. In retrospect, practically bleeding out and through my jeans in an airplane bathroom—several times over the years—was not normal. But the machine of overwork often convinces us our pain is normal, setting our standards of suffering to autopilot, set to run until we just fall down one day.

I have had six reproductive organs removed: each one died and went into the earth before the rest of my body. This was a sacrifice I made at men's altar of blood and steel and science. A sacrifice I made to keep living in this wondrous body, to keep enjoying her purpose and pleasures.

The Baba Yagas (Goddesses and grandmother spirits of Central and Eastern Europe) and other spiritual forces in my life will, in time, tell me if this sacrifice was enough to save my life, but for now, it seems yes. I am told my diagnosis was quite unusual, that I was quite young for it. It has not served me to think of it this way. I refuse the idea it is unique—especially in the great cycle of loss and grief we all live in and through now. Instead, I felt it connecting me—as if on a threshold—to an array of spirits and humans. No saccharine optimism to be found, but such aliveness poured in and through me that I had moments of feeling dazzled.

When I was in treatment, I felt I was nearly being killed to save my life. At that time, I searched the internet for books written by ovarian cancer survivors. There were few. I discovered why when I went to online ovarian cancer support groups: everyone was slowly or quickly dying in those groups except me. Most of those suffering from this cancer likely simply died before they could consider writing anything.

Then I searched for any books by women who had any kind of cancer; I found some. Many felt like sugary, optimistic fairy tales bathed in Pepto-Bismol pink. They were also overwhelmingly the stories of Christian, wealthy, white, straight women. There were also many films, books, and articles written by people who loved people with cancer and who had lost people to cancer: lovers, parents, and siblings. The lives of cancer victims and survivors impact those around us deeply, and others are often moved to speak for us. This has advantages and disadvantages, of course. We also must reserve the space and support to speak for ourselves.

This made the few books I found that were completely different all the more precious—most notably, *The Cancer Journals*, by Audre Lorde, which stands alone. She remains the only woman writer who lived with cancer I have ever read who wrote with raw truth about what it meant for her body, her sexuality, her mind, her relationships, and her children to suffer like this. She was taken from us far too soon.

As I floated in my bed, during chemotherapy, high on opioids, I deeply wanted to read (when I could read) stories. Stories I could relate to: about the raw, the eternal, the visceral, the pessimistic, the women, the queers, the dead who talk to us when we are near their realm.

I didn't want to hear the stories of praying to a God that was not mine. I was hungry to read about women grappling with cancer who were divorced, single moms, who came—as I did—from immigrant families, who had family far away, who were suffering through cancer on land that was not theirs and would never be. I did not feel the need to share every experience of these women; I just wanted to hear the pushed-out stories at the margins, which are really the stories of most of us. One in three women in the US will deal with cancer at some point in their lives, and each year there are more cancer cases among people under fifty. It seems to me some of us must chronicle the messy truths of it so that more of us can care for each other better in a time of profound alienation and isolation.

Few have written about what it is to suffer cancer surgeries and treatment during a pandemic. This experience only underscored and deepened the solitude intrinsic to all of us who come close to death, all of us who must build a new life.

I will say little explicitly in this book about my ancestral and spiritual beliefs. To say the experiences chronicled in this book "deepened my faith" would be trite. Words are magic, they help us shift power and will, and yet they fall short of what it means to know for sure where you are going when you die. It is a relief and comfort unlike any other I have ever known.

When I was a child, I was told one story about the history of the plant hemlock: one of the highest honors told in the stories of the witch burnings, was when one witch would smuggle hemlock to her tortured and imprisoned sisters. The ultimate sign of respect: allowing each to choose how much pain she wanted to take before ending her own life. At the heart of pagan Slavic belief—indigenous to Eastern Europe and part of my ancestry—are the ideas of immanence: that all things are alive and sacred. The love and the wrath of the earth are poured out upon us. Our deaths, our near deaths, our salvation, and our new lives are all catalysts for transformation in which we have some choice, some power, even when we feel we do not. There is no end, no beginning, and there never was.

I made choices in my near death. I made choices in my new life. My reasons were my own and would be different from anyone else. The book you are about to read is the book I wanted to read when I was sick. I owe a great deal to the legacy of feminist literature, particularly chronicling—the idea that it is inherently political and liberatory to chronicle painstakingly, in natural and raw time, the experiences of those who are often erased and silenced. "When we speak," Audre Lorde says, "we are afraid our words will not be heard or welcomed, but when we are silent we are still afraid, so it is better to speak remembering we were never meant to survive."

I may never fully understand this sentiment as Lorde meant it, but I know this: some books want to be born; they spew and sputter out of us like blood from a large wound. My book catapulted out of a person who was at times, barely alive. It came from a place I do not fully understand, yet it is a place that I hold sacred above all things.

I can only thank my ancestors here, and again and again eight times a year, for how they stayed close on this journey, ready for me if I were to cross over to their side. So many women in my lineage have suffered sorrow and regret silently; they urge me to speak. The honor of my life is to give voice in places they never could. I struck a deal with them: if I lived, I would write this book—for all their quiet torment and suffering that went unnamed, in home countries, on the boat over, and here on the soil of these lands.

This book is for all of us who know in our bones or seek a different way of being alive, nearing death, suffering, and even dying. It is for all of us who love someone going through these cycles. It is for all of us who want to reach beyond the numbing gauze of our times to know what suffering means, to be fully alive again, in order to be whole, again and always.

CHAPTER 1

No Saccharine Optimism, Winter 2021

I broke open, and I can tell you exactly when it started.

I did not cry when my grandmother died. It would be a long story to explain why this is a very unsettling fact. Ours was a relationship that defied conventional, white ideas of grandparents: who they are, what they mean. I lived with her; I fought with her, I stopped talking to her, I came back to her, and moved in again. My Oma (grandmother) was a force of violence, charm, deception, and humor. For many reasons, I loved her despite myself. When she died, my mother said, "You suffered her as only her own daughters suffered her." It was complicated. I knew her with an intimacy beyond most I have ever known. Almost a year after she died, I finally wrote these words through sobs that made my face swell for two days:

Every restaurant I walk into I look to see where she could sit to feel all right. She struggled so much with her size, was so ashamed of it, and her deep fear was being embarrassed in public, breaking a chair, not being able to read a certain English word, or having someone not understand her accent. Her shame was her sorrow, and her sorrow was her shame. And I was her protector, bearing that for her, concealing it for her, eating her shame, and holding it in my organs. I was her secret keeper and her ever-vigilant bodyguard. And now, loyal to a fault, I still look out for her in every seating arrangement. I see her gold-ringed fingers grip the side of the table as she sits down, the look of pain deeply carved on her face. I hear her voice asking me to comb her thin hair before we'd go out, and help her force her swollen, flaking feet into shoes. Just as she asked me, quite young, to help her write or decipher love letters to or from other women. I used to think she meant to cross boundaries, but she desperately worked with who and what she had. And now look how far down I have buried everything. I don't even speak her mother tongue to my own child, even when I say good night: I tell him his first day was my best day. But I tell him in Czech, a much more emotionally neutral language.

I have always been a secret bearer: to my grandmother, and to many other women, many of them romantic partners. Those of us who are secret bearers, pain bearers, sorrow bearers, memory bearers—we rarely want help. We are so sure of what we can bear on our own.

I was the first child born in this country to my mother's family. Like so many whose families come from afar, I carried a physical sorrow. Over time, the sorrow grows, hollowing us out, filling the empty space it creates, and settling into our body cavities.

For most of my life, I existed mostly in my head, not wanting to listen to what other parts of me had to say, hoping my mind would grow strong and dominant. Drinking helped to quiet, confuse, or stun the other parts—my spirit as well as my arms, hands, cervix, neck, shoulders, ovaries, uterus, and lower back. These last few months have been the first real conversations between these different parts of myself. They occur, in tandem, with my longest and sustained stretch of sobriety, from alcohol since I was sixteen.

•••

I have told very few people about the doctor's appointments; the pain and fatigue are still nameless. I live alone—I am the only adult and the only full-time occupant of my searingly bright little home. I live alone, suddenly, painfully, but of my own choice. This house is transitional, by definition: I have left my marital home. I've rented a small home nearby to stabilize my small son. I haven't lived alone in many years. I feel my way around the experience, arranging items and buying plants. Some days have been tumultuous, drinking too much when I don't have the child. Other days, serene but also tiring and irritating, all at once—regular life with a small child in nine hundred square feet.

One afternoon, as the sun is going down, slicing warm yellow light into the window of my cottage, I try to lift my three-year-old son into the bathtub. I struggle slightly, working to hide the effort on my face, and yet again, he sees it.

The night my son was born, I remember a long silence before he cried; the world's silence in the pause, my heart paused, hoping he would cry. Then, he did. I realized there is a moment between when a baby stops breathing water in the womb and starts breathing air. For a long moment, they don't breathe at all. Not the mother who birthed him, I walked with him to the warming table, where a nurse checked his vitals. I remember his storm blue eyes before they turned brown and his sharp and large shoulder muscles—I remember thinking he would be okay.

But now he is not sure, for reasons he does not at all understand, that I will be okay.

By that sunny afternoon, he and I had been through many upheavals. To ground us in the changes in our lives, we had a ritual of getting in the narrow, deep bathtub together, him sitting in my lap, both of us facing the drain. We would sit quietly in the bubbles as the tub filled. Play music. Sing along. It was during one of these baths that I realized I had been hiding pain. How long? The question is a porous, slippery one. What kind of pain? Feeling it in what way? I also understood that the pain may have been present without me consciously feeling it.

In general, I am not someone who wants help to care for my child. I am competent, also possessive, I suppose. This is common. There are plenty of fools walking around thinking the same thing. What a luxury, a delusion.

No human being cares for their child alone. The earth and gravity are doing much of it most of the time: filling lungs, holding up bodies, and making boundaries that children throw themselves against repeatedly. We don't even stimulate them that much. They hear the birds we have forgotten and rouse energies we no longer know. They mulch themselves in earnest joy, massaging mud and saying things like: "It's squishy. It's all squishy now." And beyond this, I have never done my share of motherhood alone either—which makes motherhood no different from anything else I have ever done.

I can see so clearly how every contribution I have ever made, politically and spiritually, was mixed with the life force of others. In fact, I rankle at anyone suggesting otherwise. Acting like social change, the building of social movements for the good of all, is a solo sport is a disservice to any possibility of the tradition of progressive change going forward in a way that could serve those coming up now and those who come after, which is pretty damn important, given the human world we are handing to them. If the next generation pursues private success and ego the way we have, they will die on the swords of individualism or, less dramatically, waste precious time.

I have been a community organizer, a popular educator, and a progressive strategist in red and purple states for my whole adult life, from the time I was twenty-one. This work has taught me a great deal and brought much joy to my life, minly through the people I have met. It also means I have learned to work well with groups. But I haven't done as well with myself and my family. For me, this has meant an adulthood of intensity, passion, debate, and delusions of self-importance.

It has been hard to follow my own advice about steering away from individualism. I was not even raising my son alone when I was well. I don't want to acknowledge this; there is this stubborn chunk in my heart, as hard as nickel, that wants, and is willing, to fence off my vulnerability—even at my son's expense. So, in the early days of my illness, I wanted him to believe that it was possible to go through cancer without pain, without knowing isolation, and filled with the deep need (sometimes unmet) for support and love. That metallic chunk, a mass that no surgery can remove, demands a heavy price. It will have to be massaged out, cried out, prayed out.

I walk around the house, and he watches me for signs of pain. Like most toddlers, he asks me every ten minutes what I am doing. He pushes me to verbalize the motions of my life. "I am reading. I am hurting. I am going to go pee. I am hurting. I am writing. I am crying. I am hurting." The next ageless and endless toddler question is, of course, "Why?" Interestingly, more and more, the answer is, "Because that is what is happening to me," or "Because that is what I want to do about how I feel," or "Because that is just how I feel." Less and less do I answer, "Because I have to."

•••

Things inside me continue to change. I get a text from a beloved friend and comrade with whom I have been in silent gridlock for almost a year. Her first sentence is, "I have started this message a million times." When I read those words, I feel an uncontrollable, feral, compulsive love for her. I do not pause to give her one moment (though she is countries away) to doubt sending her message. I write to her that I love her, that I also wish she was here. That I am not sure what is going to happen, but I know for sure I cannot be who I was before, and that means healing anything that is within my reach to heal. Right now, that means our relationship.

•••

On three sides of my cottage, I have neighbors within a hundred feet. I lie on the couch in pain and open the windows on sun-warmed afternoons, and I can hear others living, as they can hear my household doing the same. My visitors come, sit on the couch, and are taken aback at every noise. It all sounds so close in the quiet, white-hot Phoenix sun.

The dog next door sounds like he is in bed with me. He often howls of his loneliness and his sadness. When this year and my illness began, I remember moments when I envied him, how he spoke aloud, from his rusty-fenced yard to a sky—no matter what moon shone.

As my warm, wet reluctant spirit grew over these months, sometimes, I would cry with him. For the first time in my life, I would cry whenever I felt like it. I was still crying for myself, sure. But neither he nor I were crying alone.

It took time for my diagnoses to spin down in a blurring spiral, each more unexpected and difficult than the last. Medical students were placed in examination rooms with me to see how such a surprising and terrifying diagnosis is delivered to a patient. The staff dismissed for the day before the doctor talked to me. Signs I was too ignorant to notice. As that cycle of being informed ended and I moved into the next, I finally cried for my nut-brown pitbull neighbor and not for myself. For his loneliness. The cries I had after that for myself were much more genuine.

● ● ●

My body is friendly, indifferent to my many feelings. It has told me, in plain and specific terms, that it is not up for my plans, even though I have very few of them now. I have desires; I have hopes. I make very few plans because attempting to carry them out would risk my life. This feels easier because the whole country is in a COVID cocoon of loss and disconnection; collectively we are still unsure about what plans we should make for ourselves.

Between medical leaves, I go to work. My work involves listening, talking, idea generation, moving ideas along, and working to unify groups toward joint action. It involves so very many meetings. I find—interestingly—that I still absolutely love some meetings, especially the ones where I can help lay something bare for healing. I am interested in the meetings where various new and old ideas are paired and explored. I like the ones where I meet new people who voice the curiosity, intensity, and humility I feel right now. There are also some I don't like at all. The ones I do not like feel passive-aggressive and indirect, they feel like stakeouts.

In our culture, some sentences are weapons. Weapons have purpose and power, but nothing fashioned to injure others does much else well. One example is, *"You have absolutely no idea how I feel."* That sentence is one possible truth for me, a warm gun in my pocket, a chance to hurt someone, no matter how well-intentioned they are. I stand on that threshold, but I have no desire to load or fire my weapon. I throw it in the river. I turn back to the much more challenging and more arduous work of remembering, as Alice Walker wrote, that we are never the first or the last to love, suffer, or die.

I hear bloodlust in a debate, on TV, or in my many meetings, reckless injury, and the alienation of those we need on our side. I think: *It must be satisfying to think you have all the time in the world to cut instead of sew.*

I sometimes receive messages from people who describe some small concrete way my writing helped them sort something out. I find this more quietly satisfying than accolades.

On the threshold where I sit, accolades mean utterly nothing; it would be hard to overstate their lack of meaning. Meaning, beauty, and purpose remain. For the first time, I feel purpose taking a backseat to meaning and beauty.

A gentle but very sharp knife has cut what I care about away from what I do not. It has not ravaged or randomly slashed at my life; it has simply separated and put distance between ideas and dynamics I find worthy of my precious days and those I do not. I wish the peace of that knife for more of us. I walk around life, sorting, like pulling clean clothes away from dirty: that matters, that does not.

CHAPTER 2

All In, Spring 2021

I wonder strange things at night, like if the brightness under my skin exists because, nowadays, I only eat things that once swam in the sea, grew on trees, or came out of the ground. As a first-timer talking to my body's tissues, I ask if, through what we consume, they taste, digest, and remember swimming, being complete in the water. I ask if they remember salt and soil and the smell of tubers. If they remember what it is like to have roots and stretch down through them physically.

One of my former partners and dearest friends tells me that he sits on his deck at night and listens to the place where the water meets evergreens. Every time he breathes, he tries to imagine how a jellyfish moves. "I know that is weird," he says. "No," I reply, "it works for me." These days, I am asking questions I was once afraid of. I believe in the ways I did as a child but had forsaken. I am taking the entire world up on offers I used to turn down.

• • •

I wonder why I read so rarely about anyone missing their parts. I never thought about it until I began a process wherein so many pieces were being removed from my body.

They call some tumors; they call some organs. But all I know is I am in the process of losing parts of me permanently. Each of them took up space and did things (I refuse to say they "worked"). They lived, they breathed, they existed, they grew, they gave.

Some of their names sound nothing to me like what I have lost. Fallopian tubes. Uterus. Cervix. Only the word "ovaries" makes a sound in my mouth or on the page that reminds me of what I think they are. The word "ovaries" makes me think of bird sanctuaries, a home for winged ones, storage, I guess, of a sacred kind. I believe there were eggs inside my ovaries, based on phonetics alone. The doctors tell me one of my ovaries was eaten by cancer, and all the eggs inside it were eaten as well. The surgeon says that when she went to touch it in surgery, it fell apart under her knife, spilling cancer cells into the cavity of my abdomen. None of these words have any traction in the muddy terrain of my heart. They get stuck and make no sense. I am a storyteller, a truth-teller, a framer, and a writer. So, I rewrite this report: *My eggs were poisoned, their home was poisoned, and the poison burst and spread in the big sanctuary under my ribs. Knives cut and pulled out some poison and pieces of me, and now there is a hollow space inside for me to fill and more poison to heal from.*

Hipsters call tracks of music "deep cuts" nowadays. It sounds like marketing to a generation who wants to feel something deep and meaningful, even if it hurts. When you have been cut a great deal, music is music. Deep is deep. Shallow is shallow. You don't want to cut or be cut more than necessary.

I am told I can live with pieces removed from the whole of my body. I believe that. They expect me to be grateful, and in many ways I am. Still, several parts of myself have already died and returned to where the whole came from. How do we change when we lose so many organs all at once? I wonder if this is why I feel the ancestors behind and in me. They bump around in my cottage, like an over-crowded house party. All these ancestors, all these dead—because parts of me are already dead and buried. I shudder thinking of my precious pieces in a plastic medical waste bag. A biohazard. How comical—that my poisoned parts are now a hazard to the earth. "Just not plastic," I think to myself. "No synthetic barrier between my parts and the earth." That would be sacrilege, the kind of sacrilege most of us commit every day, throwing dead flowers and apple cores and beetroot into plastic bags to go in landfills when they cry out to live again as good, rich black soil. Yet, no prophylactics, no plastic bags, is not a bad goal for the rest of me that still lives as well: remove the barrier, get in the soil, move around.

In the past, I never cared enough about my body to worry or think about its parts. The whole glorious, organic concoction of my body was just a vehicle to answer to my drive, ambition, and will. Now, however, I seek out the best yellow and green Thai curries in town. I can taste the difference for the first time. I would have told you I could before, but I assure you I did not.

• • •

When you have surgeries during a pandemic, you must go alone. You get dropped off and are given a plastic bag to put your ID and other shit in. This is to ensure they don't lose your belongings in the shuffle. Even kids must go alone at a certain point, their eyes flat and stunned, holding their bags in their little hands. Patients don't look each other in the eyes in the waiting room. The most I ever mustered was to say to the guy in the wheelchair beside me, "You think they wouldn't put *ER* reruns on the TV in here." He laughed. Then we both managed to croak "Good luck" as they wheeled him away.

You don't look at each other in the beds, in the hospital gowns, waiting, with the IVs in. Most people seem to be on their phones, scrolling, waiting. I can't bring myself to do that. I lie there and struggle to remember what I promised myself: I am the only one here, so it is my job to love myself as others would if they were with me. Love me without hesitation, ambivalence, or remorse; without scrutiny or judgment. It's a tall order, but, in reality, the only person who can love me through this is me. There are no other options. No one else can cross the threshold. How many learned this before me? How many are facing this right right—I mean right *now*?

• • •

In *The Cancer Journals*, Audre Lorde wrote, "I do not wish my anger and pain and fear about cancer to fossilize into yet another silence, nor to rob me of whatever strength can lie at the core of this experience, openly acknowledged and examined."[1]

Like many feminist twenty-year-olds, I read *The Cancer Journals* in a college class. I feel affection and amusement for the part of me that thought I knew what it was about.

I did not.

I also have affection for the thirty-nine-year-old, who now also thinks she understands it. Very possibly, I understand only one small part of it.

• • •

Two things happen, and at first they feel unrelated. One is that, as I mentioned, people I don't know reach out and

---

1. Audre Lorde, *The Cancer Journals* (San Francisco: Aunt Lute, 1997), 7.

tell me that something I wrote mattered to them, helped them, guided them, stayed with them. I honestly find this shocking. This is not false modesty. It is more feral. I have written from the hilt, on the fly, my whole life. It may be the one thing I do or embody where I trust instinct and inspiration completely. More than sex, more than mothering, more than work. So, I do find it hard to believe it has given so much to others. Perhaps, like so many people raised as "women," I learned early that, if any activity pleased me or made me come alive, was organic and unfettered and raw, it must be of no use to the world. It must be for me alone and therefore shameful. I came to believe I should do fewer activities like this. They couldn't possibly be generative.

As I am written to about my writing, I start taking to my bed in the afternoons, high as a kite on opioids, with a mini-speaker and books. I read Lorde, Rilke, Rich, Rumi. . . just everything that felt right that I could get my hands on. I order books constantly. I peel and devour poetry and music and prose in bed like the sack of clementines in the kitchen that I can no longer eat and I weep whenever it gets me good, just like I did my whole damn childhood. And I think how good it is what these writers made, and how it turns out I needed each piece so much, not *even* now, but more now, and now, and again.

Rilke wrote the first part of *The Book of Hours* at twenty-one for the thirty-six-year-old married Russian woman he loved crazily, a love that fulfilled him for a lifetime, though they were lovers for a relatively brief time. And I think, fuck, of course, he did. People always think he wrote it about God. Which, of course, he did. And he also wrote it for the stone-cold fox who taught him what being alive is.

And thus, I back myself into caring about writing again, caring very much. And once I start to care about writing again—the crushing, elusive, blood-and-guts glory of it—I care to write again as well.

•••

I dream I am a teenager in a house with floors of almond-colored wood. I am sitting on the threshold between the kitchen and the living room. The dead are cooking. The living are busy in the living room. I am waiting to carry bowls of borscht (that shade of glowing magenta) from the kitchen to the living room.

Due to my life-threatening illness, and what I am told are my limited chances of long-term survival (15 percent)—my threshold is sharp and clear, highlighted in neon-like text in a poetry book. But last year's circle of seasons set all of us, packed tightly, at the very same threshold. My time feels finite around me; I have a gift that comes with a breathtaking price—seeing myself and others more clearly. This is new: previously, my blessing and curse were to see myself and those I love mainly as what we can be, can do, and can make possible. Though a gift in organizing, this often creates struggle in one's personal life.

So, I look with new eyes (not a new lens, but wet, remade eyes, eyes my son would call squishy) and feel a friendliness to those around me, unreached before. It wells up in me, not summoned by formidable will, my oldest friend. I think to myself, I want more of this feeling. I don't want it to end. I want it for more than just me.

Swimming in seas of all things privatized, numb, and individual, our times make our own shapes more difficult to feel. We're overstimulated but spiritually starving. But this living from within outward can allow us to push out new bulbs, leaves, and flowerings, and, in doing so, the rotted, the addictive, the stuck matter can be pushed out of us. There is no nobility in how I change; I simply am new growth because the old has run out of space on the branch.

The day comes in my illness when I burn everything in the house that is for burning: candles, grasses, incense. I use all the bath salts in the hall closet and slather my stitched and scarred little body with balms and almond oil. No holding back. No puritan impulse to preserve half bottles or boxes. I pray with complete abandon and no self-consciousness. I don't worry about doing it right: I know, as I have known nothing before, that my gods hear me. I hold the sweet back of my baby's neck up to my teeth, and I tell him every day that I love him forever, that I love him in a place that never fucking ends. He smiles rascally, because I said fucking. Each day I eat something incredibly delicious. I wear short shorts and get tan on my skinny knees and thighs. I Am All In.

CHAPTER 3

Grateful and Ungrateful, Spring 2021

*In May 2021, I began a course of chemotherapy that contin-
ued through the summer of 2021. During this time, I was isolated from most of my daily life, and aligned with the shut-in
cadences of the raging plague experienced by the whole world. I
was incredibly fortunate that my blood and chosen family came,
one after another, to help take care of me over the months. I
was incredibly fortunate to have a partner who made loving
me through something like this look easy and a core group of
dear friends locally who saw me through. Yet, I often did not
feel grateful.*

Though doctors do not talk explicitly about my chances
of survival, it does look like my chance will be pretty good
if I can get through chemotherapy. This is fresh news to
me, and it dawns on me slowly, strangely, and in stages. It is
incredibly strange, in a matter of mere months, to go from
thinking you are perfectly healthy and that you might get
pregnant and birth a baby, to understanding that you have
a cancer that kills around 85 percent of its victims, and then
to believing you might survive only by enduring poisoning
that brings you quite close to death.

Before this round of chemotherapy, I lived most of my
life in a state of seeing myself as fully alive, without feeling

particularly anxious about death. I move to an understanding and acceptance that I will likely die very soon—it is unclear if I am headed to hospice or chemotherapy. I enter isolation, near seclusion, treatment, and pain that make me feel half-deadness, undeadness, and dead/aliveness. It does not seem viscerally believable that I will survive the torment of treatment. I am awed by how little I know about those who have survived something like this—something like this kind of cancer—and how they have done it.

I quickly realize that as a previously able-bodied person, I have understood absolutely nothing about disability, illness, drug use, or cancer itself. Until this, I have had no idea what chemotherapy does to my body—just as, previously, I had no idea what the aftermath of three surgeries would mean for it, and still have no idea what early and radical menopause will mean for me physically, spiritually, emotionally, or sexually.

It becomes clear after only one round of chemotherapy that my bone marrow will not be able to withstand another five without bone marrow injections. These injections, coming twenty-seven hours after each round of chemotherapy, are commonly prescribed and cause incredible pain because they trigger bone marrow cells to grow again after chemotherapy ravages them. This is a very sobering scientific miracle—or travesty, depending on your point of view. Your bones are told, "Wake up! Remember when we were a baby, a toddler, a small child, and we grew bones? We need to do that again. We need to do it today. And, in twenty-one days, I will push you to do it all over again."

I now have between ten and twenty hot flashes a day, around the clock, day and night. As a person who has always allowed life to change me, politicize me, and transform me, I am politicized by what I am quickly learning. I have always trusted most how life politicizes us: experiences, people, and places transform us more than concepts alone.

Books have politicized me only to the extent they speak to me of experiences, people, places, and feelings. I found my queerness through glances, feelings, looking back on moments and newly understanding them. I came to trust myself this way; I came to forgive myself for my own denial and delusion this way (viscerally) as well.

Aside from Lorde, nothing I *read* about cancer politicizes me, but some of it confirms and validates my experiences and makes me feel less alone. However, *writing* about it does politicize me. It frees me: I feel unselfconscious and raw in the written and shared word. I was raw in my writing in the past, but not in my editing. As an editor I was always ruthless, obsessively critical, and negative. It was as though, throughout my whole life, I was most myself when writing, but as soon as I became my own editor, I hated myself the most. Now, though, I create space for what I put on the page, and my internal editor allows it.

I have a few friends who have been through cancer, and the ones my age are so traumatized it is hard to be sober and up for talking at the same time. I have sought books that fulfill my need to feel less alone. There are few. Anne Boyer's *The Undying* is powerful, partially because she is an artist and a single mom. But Audre Lorde reaches me the most. Perhaps this is a sacrilege to say, but I can feel her cancer and how the urgency shaped her writing. I feel all of it: the frantic fight to have energy, her fragmentation, the intense effort to document herself, the denial. I can sense, even without knowing the history and context, how much less space she had in her life than me to write. I can tell she was doing a million things at once. I am not right now; I am only doing *this*.

I feel in awe of how few women with cancer have written what they have been through and had it published. It is objectively appalling, given that almost one in three women will deal with cancer in our lifetimes. Most of the

literature that I find feels like it found its way to recognition and audience through experiences, stories, and energies
that are nothing at all like what I am going through. Much
of it feels so saccharine, so positive, pink-ribboned, white,
straight, and suburban. It is sugarcoating things that are not
and should not taste sweet. It focuses on those around the
cancer patient: how they feel and what they need. There are
a lot of stories about healthy people who have loved people
with cancer—who had mothers, partners, children who suffered cancer. When I first realized this, bitterness filled my
mouth. I am sure the people around us have much to say;
their lives are transformed by cancer as well. But they seem
to have much more space to tell their stories. Perhaps, it is
because we are more tired, bitter, in more pain, or because,
at least with ovarian cancer, we just die quickly and quietly.

I attend online support groups for women with ovarian
cancer. I feel awkward and voyeuristic because I am at least
twenty years younger than everyone else there—and the
only person not actively dying/prolonging life. I am the only
one with a "good" prognosis. I realize that, before cancer, I
was struggling deeply with empathy; I wanted to feel it for
years; I said I felt it, but I was numb to my pain and the
pain of others. Empathy came back to me all at once. There
was a day that I doubled over weeping as I had a vision of a
hundred chairs where people with ovarian cancer sat. I sat
in one of the fifteen chairs that held the survivors. In this
vision, I could not find the other fourteen long-term survivors or talk to them. The other eighty-five chairs emptied
as, one by one, everyone else died.

I write for myself, and I write for the ones who can't and
would want me to do so. I write for her because she put off
going to the doctor when she saw the signs; she was too
busy caring for others. I write for him, who put off going
to the doctor, because they would call him a freak for even
having ovaries. I write for the woman who wanted to go to

a doctor, bleeding month after month through her pants, but was too broke, without insurance, and working every waking moment of her damn life. I write for her, who went to the doctor, and it was already too late—she had come to a fork in the road and was sent to hospice or home, not to chemotherapy. I write for her in my cancer group, who had a hundred tumor markers returned, yet said she wanted to enjoy her dogs and a picnic at a lake and one last summer. I write for the brilliant and dead women, the queers, all dead too soon, who may have written a book a shitload better than this one but never will. I chronicle the pain, the mess, the drugs, everything: to say that it matters. What happens to us matters because someone who can do it should honor it enough to write about every raw, ragged detail.

During my weeks of chemotherapy, I think a lot about women and cancer, anger and cancer, silence and cancer, class and cancer, race and cancer. I think about queer and trans people and cancer. I regularly visit the colossal fortress of cancer, the Mayo Clinic, rising out of the desert on the outskirts of Phoenix. I bow down when told to be grateful to get care there: a shrine of efficient healing, a machine of empire and money, a beehive of near-death numbness. I do feel grateful sometimes. And sometimes not at all. I am surrounded in the fortress mostly by elderly white people, everyone looking straight and straitlaced—no one looking anyone in the eye. Over time, I grow precise at smelling and feeling which of my fellow patients are near death.

To withstand chemotherapy—particularly the high dose prescribed for younger people who are more likely to survive—I have to aggressively advocate for my own long-term opiate use that often leaves me numb, eerily quiet, and despondent. I have to be aggressive because, due to the greed of pharmaceutical companies, Arizona has just passed new opioid laws that make it hard for everyone to access them, even those who need them to survive the pain of cancer treatment. The same drugs that allow me to continue treatment also give me monthly withdrawals; as I finish each ten-day round of chemotherapy, with poison still in my veins, I struggle to swim toward some strange form of sobriety.

During this time, I write and write and write whenever I am able. I write this book. I often write into it around two or three a.m. As pain wakes me, I take more opiates and have an hour or so as I wait for them to kick in. Or I wake up and need to wait another hour before it is safe to take more.

Doctors and chemo ward chaplains tell patients to "commit to your treatment" repeatedly. In the beginning, not knowing how much agony was to come, these instructions made no sense to me. As my treatment goes on, I understand; if you didn't remember why you are committed to the treatment, it would be almost impossible to continue.

In the middle of the night, sweating in my underwear, even that commitment does not feel like enough. I grasp onto the idea of unfurling my spine and taking responsibility for myself and my choice to live through the times we find ourselves in—times of turning, unraveling, unmaking, vast endings, and changes beyond comprehension. I remind myself, "Yes. I want to live in a time of fire and floods and slow and fast death. I want to live through my son's childhood, to uncover the mundane and glorious world with him."

I consciously decide to work to live, to do all I can. My reasons are local; they live in my own heart and mind. I choose life in a time when so many around me, suicide in all obvious and unobvious ways. A time of apocalypse, in the oldest definition of the word. As best as I could, I began to honor the responsibility of choosing the raw, army crawl, beyond all boundaries of civility, within and through cancer.

● ● ●

In "Uses of the Erotic," Audre Lorde writes: "When we begin to live from within outward. . . then we begin to be responsible for ourselves in the deepest sense."[2] I believe she means that we are responsible for ourselves as all of one piece, a whole. This idea differs from "accountability," implying calculating, collecting, and correcting.

As our social maladies shift and rearrange just as the pandemic keeps changing, we have difficulty meeting each other's eyes. We don't know what to ask of each other; we don't know what to expect. Maybe we sense that we could come at each other differently, in new ways, but we are unsure how to do so. Our cells are literally out of practice at relations. We went into our wintering, millions of us thinking we had roots and intimacies that were deeper than reality proved them to be. It took several months before we were humbled into gratitude for who and what we *do* have.

"Accountability," weaponized and bearing great consequence, has been a vital tool in unmaking and remaking worlds, bringing about social change. Far more people today can finally hold humans who were previously unreachable accountable for their actions. Bringing accountability to powerful humans who have done great, great harm is incredibly positive. We can see it every day in digital spaces, where so much of our world making and unmaking happens. The problem with the word is that it bears the fruit of a tree with its roots in "counting."

When we turn the word "accountable" against each other, in public or private, it does what it was conjured to do from the first: it counts. It counts our merits. If our pains, struggles, intense and complex secrets, and profound failings mark us as irredeemable, it counts us out. Our visible

---

2. Audre Lorde, "Uses of the Erotic: The Erotic as Power," in *Sister/Outsider: Essays and Speeches* (Berkeley,: Crossing Press, 2007), 58.

failures—not the ones that no one knows, the ones that keep us up at night—are also tallied. Ultimately, the trouble with "accountability" is that only our actions, isolated from all else, count. We arrive before the judge and jury—stripped, shivering, de-contexted, and wait to be numbered, counted, convicted, and discarded. Accountability is powerful. Despots and dictators will be dethroned, harm will be reduced, and some will be brought to the only forms of justice our sick society can accept and metabolize. But accountability will not help us change forms, individually or collectively. We will not jump off the death-cult hamster wheel into the great abyss of uncertainty with grace.

Trust me on this or don't, but looking right into the eyes of my death—not anyone's death, but my personal one—being accountable means jack shit to me. It has fallen away. Count me, or don't. Think of counting whether I am good enough or not. As I suffer to save my own life, I turn away from accountability for this lifetime (no matter how much longer or shorter it might be) and turn to *responsibility*.

The word "responsibility" does not have roots in its present-day connotations. It currently implies adulthood, a dull virtue, connected to doing what is right but unappealing. But its real roots are in the verb "to respond." It is based on the idea of someone being "answerable" to a question, idea, or task. Lorde's responsibility for oneself asks who and what I am answerable to and where are the places I am called to respond. All too often, we act as if responding to each other to what calls us, takes too much energy. I tell myself all the time that I don't have to respond to everyone, to everything, to every ask or need. I tell others the same. It doesn't help me change my form and ways that much.

What has helped me change is answering the question of who and what I answer. I have my answers. They do not always have to be put into words, but knowing them inside can help us to take the days as they come.

I *can* say that turning to responsibility and away from accountability has not made my pack light. Some days, my steps are heavy from the weight, others they are light. But every day, it is mine; I know why and how far I am willing to carry it. It is not the life I saw for myself; it is not one I chose. Yet, in each choice was the internal organic design that led me further on my path. The day I lay it down, I know where *I* will lie down. Some parts of me are in that soil already.

I wish to publicly write and talk about the responsibilities that connect me to other humans. Through grace and rawness, my beloved community has shown me the risks they have taken on me, the person they have taught me to be, and the secrets they have given me to carry. They make me whole. They create spaces for me to understand where I come from, where I walk, and where I am going. In calling their names, I am replanted, regrounded, and healed from isolation. Life returns to my numb and tingling fingers when others grip them tightly.

• • •

My friend Dori Midnight said to me during the early days of my cancer, "I sense your shape changing from something like an arrow to something more like a bowl." An arrow is created to be focused on a sole purpose. Its shape speaks of its purpose. That purpose—to pierce and kill—doesn't make me particularly uncomfortable. For a long time, I thought of progressive social change and my work to remake the world as destroying harmful systems, accomplished through building power. Systems built to destroy all that I love (and those whom I love) cannot be accepted. I still believe that. However, someone who has changed into the shape of a bowl enacts that belief very differently than someone who is shaped like an arrow. I feel the urge to build new things, be a host, welcome others in, and enter unfamiliar places.

I want to see people make the change. Differently, I want to leave orthodoxies behind, walk away from the experts in my ear, coast out, and listen more. I want to say the real thing, the true thing, and get wild and wide about how I embody a bowl. I close my eyes on a burning hot summer day in Phoenix, as the chemo under my skin makes the sun burn every part of my body, and I see a broad, clay, earthen bowl with bright clear water pouring into it until it overflows continuously. Parts of my body and shape that I have lost wash away in the overflow: hair, nails, doubts. By the time the water is running clean, it is flowing from me into my work, into my words, into my love for my son, out and out and out.

●●●

Those who speak up and are sometimes heard often speak about the cycles of how we remake the world and ourselves very abstractly. But, closer to death, we know it is more tactile, visceral, and concrete. We want cigarettes, smooth sheets, and a fan pointed at us on a stifling day. Perhaps, all of us deserve a seer who can see our current shapes and the shapes we are changing into. In every conflict, in every brutal moment, they could whisper to us about the forms we have taken and the forms we are letting ourselves become. I grunt in pain and mutter to myself: "I am becoming the bowl overflowing. It didn't come from me. It passes through me. Let it flow into me and through me. Let it flow into me and through me."

In my case, perversely, it helps a lot when I look in the mirror; I'm always reassured by the symmetrical tattoos on my arms, fingers, and back, even though I can never explain why I've acquired them. I see people of a certain age ordering from Instagram ads and conjuring every kind of tattoo possible, all trying to look unique but looking all the same. Others change their eyes, lips, breasts, and cheeks, making them all look identical. Now beauty means making our faces unable to bend into shapes that show our emotions. I think, ah, kids, but when you look different—marked—you might not want that. When you're bald like lightning hit you—a cautionary tale: be careful what you wish for.

I am without a hair, except my once beautiful and full eyebrows, now thinned, once two twin sources of vanity, discernment, and pride on my forehead. I wear head coverings with patterns of Slavic flowers. There's a look in my eyes: blown out, the eyes of someone who has seen stars explode inside her body. People stare at me from the corners of their eyes. Though I love one-on-one attention, I have never liked being someone everyone looks at when they enter a room. I say to my mother, laughing, "Jesus, I look really out there. I think I would like just to wear gray and brown clothes."

Looking "really out there." Like someone from a far, far shore. I might look like an oracle from a movie. Yes, a hermit oracle, a witch on an island, from the part in the film where the sailors come to her cave and she gives them the next step: the insight, the vision. Then they leave. But what happens to her?? Who is she before and after? What does she do with her days and nights—is she lonely, is she tortured, is she content? Or perhaps I look quite like that one ancestor that two different seers, strangers from entirely different traditions, cultures, and geographies, saw near me. All they told me was that she was old, and that she covered her head in dark cloth. I have been trying to figure out who she is: surely from the Slavic side, the side of my mother's father, the side my mother favors in her face. She is not me, but perhaps I now resemble her.

•••

I feel myself changing shape. I have hunched over much of my life, even though I am tall and have broad shoulders. It is a shape I have practiced myself into, and it still comes readily. Looking for the gaps, failings, and holes in everyone and everything is also a shape we practice ourselves into. We have our reasons, but repetition wins the day, the week, the month, the year. We are creatures of habit. Suddenly, mirrors and reflective glass became difficult for me, and, for the first time, I understood the possible reasons certain Jewish days of mourning call for covered mirrors.

When asked how I am, I often respond that I am not in good shape. This actually strikes me as a falsehood, as I write it. I am in a new shape, or form. I am not ready to look at that shape or see it yet.

•••

On the days I feel good, I feel so damn good. I wonder if I feel better than those around me. Many have spent the long seasons of the pandemic secluded and scared, questioning anything and everything—segmented, separated, lacking reference, and surrounded by sudden, devastating loss in a dominant culture that teaches us almost nothing useful about navigating loss, grief, and confusion. We are beings that suffer cellular and tissue trauma from being isolated. It affects our balance, our brains, our immune systems, our nervous systems, and, of course, our spirits. Yet, we try to ignore these effects and "move on." We have shared a plague and had a collective near-death experience to some extent. It is simply that some of us know we have had one and some of us don't. Some of us are ready, or at least able, to be present, and others are not. Perhaps, the generality of this global specter of death is hard to absorb. But we shared the risks, to different degrees, of one plague. He came with one face, he came with one name, he came over one wind.

My death is not a he. Her face is known to me, defying description and yet quite clear to me. Her name remains unknown; she may just as well be named Cancer as not. Her presence has permanently altered the rest of my life. Her accompaniment changes that which I am in ways hard to describe—making me older and not older. A traditional and ancient pagan European understanding of the life cycle is symbolized in the immanence of the Goddess herself: She is Maiden, she is Mother, and then she is Crone. In moments when it is hard to continue for myself, mothering drives me forward in my treatment and its agonies. I am willing to suffer this for myself as well, but the urgency and intensity of my treatment are supported by mornings spent with my face in my son's chubby, dirt-covered toddler hands. It is not as simple as wanting to live for him. It is more that the intensity of our intimacy pushes me along the poison cycle, hoping to get back to the regular, annoying and sacred work of mothering as soon as possible. To live the bargain I struck meant I could no longer produce a new life, at least not a baby, inside of me. Instead, I am destined to learn about the other ways humans make and nurture new life.

The sacrifices I have made are, thus, very concrete. I am a woman who lingered a long time as a Maiden. I loved being one. I loved the adventure and the ability to commit entirely to my life work. It aligned with my desire to focus obsessively, solely, and in a place luxuriously afield from the rest of my life. Looking down at the jeans, boots, and backpack, jumping on the train. On mornings that I didn't know or care much about how the nights ended up—I was along for the ride. I lived and moved in great pleasure and freedom, fighting the good fight, crossing the ocean that separates my motherland and fatherland, quite literally. I crisscrossed language and culture and family, navigating both sides. I held a heavy spirit, but my able, resourced, and supported body was light.

How I experienced the feral joy of motherhood later in life shocked me; I expected to be ambivalent and was profoundly not so. On day three of my son's life, I held him over the wooden kitchen table; the sky glowed, ever so slowly, over the grapefruit tree in the yard before dawn. His eyelids were closed and swollen; beneath them his eyes were still milky and unfocused. He was terrifying, so demanding, confusing, and tiny. A sleep robber, a drainer of my solitary will, a life changer, a bearer of a permanent commitment I had never known. I said aloud to him and the spirit world, "I am yours for as long as I am here, and you are deeply wanted. You are mine and ours—I claim you." Since that moment, that intimacy has been definitive for me. So many of us say to our children, "For you, there is nothing I would not do." But life calls each of us to live that statement so differently. Some know what it means to walk out on that promise, to cross borders previously unknown. That promise taught me my limits, with its rosy and bold truth and simultaneous naïveté. Because there are limits, of course, to how much pain I would be willing to live with. Only people like the one I used to be—people who have not borne pain beyond endurance—think otherwise.

But if you ask me for specifics about what I would be willing to do to see my precious ancestral homeland again, hear the pines whisper to me and me alone on a train headed east to Poland from Berlin, or what I would do to be able to see my son become an awkward twelve-year-old, I can tell you, with specifics. And the truth is I would suffer a great, great deal.

For the promise of these moments, I would put fire in my veins. I would allow chemotherapy made from the poison of a Yew Tree to run through every river, pond, and tributary of my blood. I would endure a pain in my hip bones, knees, ankles, and feet that only a Baba Yaga of great age feels. I picture her, weighed down by the gravity of being a mediator and arbitrator in the world, not above it but rooted in the earth's center. A bone pain so great you try endlessly to rest or walk when you can do neither.

There is nothing romantic about this. Clarity does not mean relief. But I am not confused about what I am willing to do to be in this body, this form, for another round. I am also unconfused about my death, her coming, her presence, my hopes that my sacrifices have won me more time before she comes for me. I am not afraid of her anymore.

The stories of Baba Yaga, the Grandmother Witch, existed for hundreds of years in stories before she was ever written down, different in every Slavic language and land, but always with some shared qualities. She is sometimes a villain, sometimes a life-affirmer and giver. She is a decider, providing salvation only for those willing to transform completely. In a picture book from my childhood, she lives in a house that stands on chicken feet, a home always turning around in a circle. To some she appears "deformed," to others, ferocious—but she is always an enigma, an ambiguous figure.

A Baba Yaga is an ambivalent life-mother; she gives life, and she exacts it. She is an eater, a taker, a giver. She mediates the boundary of death. She can kill you, cook you; she can spare you. But she never spares without a test, without a sacrifice, without you coming back new. Changed is the only way she lets you return—she eats those unwilling to sacrifice. When I talk about a sacrifice, there is no saccharine, American chaser involved. The sacrifice Baba Yaga demands is not easy: it is not a sacrifice unless it shakes you to the core, unless you are no longer the person you were before you made it.

• • •

After a long maidenhood, I am in the limbo between Mother and Crone, moving in my body as the first, a body subjected to the hot flashes, rages, and new sensations of the second. Before my surgeries, after decades of painful periods, I longed to bleed in the ground one more time. I chuckled as I got my wish, camping, at 2 a.m., under a half moon and Sedona pines. What a pain in the ass. I sit up in the cold night watching the cold sky for an hour.

CHAPTER 4

The Underworld Time, Summer 2021

As it does for millions of others, chemotherapy (and the opioid use accompanying it for me) changed who I was for the duration of my treatment. What I did not know, but other cancer survivors will recognize, is that chemotherapy and its impact are cumulative, so I deteriorated as the summer went on. Spiritually, I entered a space where I was often silent, staring into the space between the dead and the living. I decided to write when I was high on opiates and when I was not. It was part of a commitment to honor my personhood, my aliveness, no matter what shape I was in. When I was in pain and when I was numb. There were also weeks when I was in so much pain, that I did not write.

Two relationships have become definitive for me: one to cancer and one to death. At first, they felt entwined. Now that I have begun the fire-and-lightning treatment of chemotherapy, they feel more separate. In my relationship with cancer, I must crawl through a summer of heat and cycles of pain to get to my prognosis. A prognosis that, if I commit to all my treatment, is generally good. The word "good" is so vague, but one that wily doctors use consistently and stubbornly. However, the prognosis is not in my sweaty little hands now; I still have a long way to go until it can be mine.

My relationship with the prospect of death is very different than it once was; it has no season. There is no shiny prize to crawl to. The specter is in me, around me; its face is known to me, its story in me. Death feels near to me now, close, not frightening, but changing.

I crack myself up one afternoon thinking about the irony and ego of imagining I have things to say to a world coming out of its grueling isolation, as I continue to be very isolated by my circumstances. Perhaps it is precisely because I must save my life consciously and messily, at great pain and cost that I "get to" ask awkward, difficult questions like, "Who among us still wants to live with, in, and through such times? And if so, in what ways?" Before cancer, I may have asked, "Live to do what? To produce what?" But now I would simply ask, "And live how?"

In the early stages of my illness, when my diagnoses were in free fall, I cycled through a great deal of joy and empathy for all those around me. There was also a lot of adrenaline. There's a time when your world of people first learns you are sick when everyone is in touch with you. Then there is a time in illness when most people you know, most acquaintances, mostly forget about you and go about their day-to-day lives. I have regularly done the same for others, so I get it. Summer 2021 is that time for me. Still, I have many people in my life who have not forgotten me, who love me better, with more skill, than I ever have them. As I get sicker and balder and brighter, my world gets smaller. Yet the people in it are so radiant to me, so messy, looming large in my small world, meaning very much to me as they care for me and walk with me.

•••

My son wakes at midnight, furious and screaming—normal three-year-old stuff, not weird cancer tantrum stuff. He is pissed off because the last thing he remembers is happily driving in the car with my sister and me after late evening babysitter pick-up. I hated picking him up at 8 p.m., but chemotherapy ruled my day, so we drove him home, looking at lights until he was asleep. He does not remember being put to bed, tucked in, and kissing good night. He stands at his toddler gate, shaking with fury screaming *mommy mommy mommy*, which is not the name this child with two mothers has ever called me. *Mina* is what he usually calls me, a contraction of a common Slavic word *Maminka* which means mother. But now he calls *mommy mommy mommy*—shrieking to be mothered.

And yet, when I take the eight quick steps to the gate, he is so furious I was not there with him to start with that he won't let me in. When he does, he hits my naked thighs repeatedly. I tell him that I must go back to the other room if he hits me. This is an example of the huge divide between the (temporarily) healthy and the very ill, not a thought-out parenting tactic but a physical fact. I am the only parent in this house and I had chemotherapy today. If he continues to hit me, I will bruise severely, so I will have to go back to my room. The toddler gate, ironically, literally protects my fragile body from my forty-pound beloved. He stops hitting me, his eyes closed, crying and crying. He hits the mat that I use to lie down with him; he hits my knit yellow blanket. He kneels down, striking out at things that represent me since he can't hit me. After a few minutes he stops and buries his head in my yellow blanket smelling me and sobbing but still not accepting the hand I reach out to him. Then, without looking at me, he crawls into his bed and goes back to sleep. I think to myself: I get it; I feel like that all the time. Emotions rage through me, striking out at what and where I can and then crawling back to bed.

When he has a tantrum, I go to words—answering his words with other words when he is just pure emotion and neurons firing. I try to dialogue and reason. Often, though, what he needs is presence, a quiet voice, to be held, or to reject being held but not be abandoned.

In the hot, stinging, tropical-storm waves of emotion that make up the bodies of water called *ovarian cancer, queerness, motherhood, radical menopause, whiteness, immigration, divorce, and new love*, mostly what I feel is intense pain, and no dialogue helps me much either. After his tantrum, his snoring starts. I cannot sleep. My body is filled with steroids. He started screaming at midnight and was asleep again by 12:15. I started writing this on the back of a UPS box, by the light of the open microwave oven.

• • •

I used to have a menstrual cycle that was finally regular after more than a year of not traveling during the pandemic. Now, at thirty-eight (I think I am thirty-eight, I cannot count well these days), I do not have one and will never have one again. I now have a chemo cycle. My menstrual cycle was filled with different stages: ovulating, unexpected spotting, heavy bleeding, and cramps. My chemo cycle moves from unbearable physical pain to severe emotional pain, to feeling strangely steady but unhealthy, and back to unbearable pain. The kind of chemo I take into my vein six to eight hours at a time, comes from a poison yew tree. It is too toxic to touch my skin. Before chemotherapy, a plastic tube is forced into my vein to protect all the layers of my skin from having contact with it. The nurses put on hazardous-materials smocks and gloves, marked with warning symbols that look like props for a zombie movie.

After the forced IV and stent, four separate drugs are forced through my veins (with saline flushes between each one) before my body is ready to receive the poison of the yew tree without completely rejecting it. The first two are fifty milligrams of Benadryl followed by a mainlined steroid. Like me, you probably have no idea what it means to experience this combination. A nurse gave me a good metaphor for the impact: "If your body were a car, it would feel like you were hitting the gas and the brake at the same time." This is exactly how it feels.

Finally, after an hour of pre-meds, I lie into the chemoward recliner and let the tree called yew poison me. I fall into a stupor, picturing its trunk and branches. Yew is an ancient tree that grows in many places but grows old and big and strong in my ancestral homeland of Central and Eastern Europe. It is a tree that guards graveyards and can hollow but not die; it can live again, a tree of death, life, and resurrection. Its age is often difficult to determine, and it is so poisonous that generation after generation of humans tells their children: do not touch it, do not eat it. And the few that history remembers who do usually use it to take their own lives intentionally. It can live for thousands of years. It grows more horizontally than vertically: its branches reach for the ground around it, not the sky above it. Since the drug Taxol was approved for the treatment of ovarian cancer and advanced breast cancer in the early 1990s, the yew tree has become a victim of intense exploitation: China is growing millions of trees to sell. I have considered buying one to keep in my house, but I fear it would poison my son. The irony forces a bitter chuckle.

The yew makes me dream strange things in the chair. I dream I am on a boat with my sister, rocking. when I am more sober, I tell my sister, "I wanted to ask you why are we on this big ship?" Later the same night, my sister says that she believes our family brought all its ancestral wisdom and trauma over on "the boat" my mother, her sisters, and her parents came over on. Only then do I realize that the yew dream took me on the ship that my mother sailed in as a scared girl. My sister was there with me. The actual ship voyaged for four weeks, and my mother's story about watching the whales eat the garbage thrown overboard appears over and over in my head.

Using your mind to convince your body to be poisoned is complicated and gradual. For days after my first infusion, I felt a lightning in my veins and pains that forced me to walk around hunched over (when I could walk at all) like the Baba Yaga herself. I find myself bargaining, coming up with reasons I don't have to go to the next chemotherapy appointment. Patients ghost those appointments all the time, and I understand why. To ghost: to not appear, to leave only the smoky suggestion of where you could have been, but you are not—suggesting those already dead.

I have heard this resistance to showing up for treatment compared to how those in the act of childbirth say they just wanted to get up and leave—your body thinking: if I can just leave this place, I won't feel this pain. In the place where they poison me, naturally, many others are being "consensually" poisoned. Most of them are much older than me, with fewer tattoos than me, apparently straighter than me, bald like me, white like me. Sometimes I feel like I am in a faux US when I am in the Mayo Clinic: the country the far right wants this to be—filled only with the white, the straight, the bland. Yet, they are not young and not able-bodied, and they are not friendly, even to each other. If I must be tortured, I would rather be tortured in a place that looks more like the country that I actually live in: young, old, queer, straight, white, of color, tatted up, straitlaced, transient, settled, broke, rich, laughing, crying, yelling, and quiet.

Unlike me, the others at Mayo each have a small but mostly white entourage, though sometimes they are alone. I still don't look in their eyes, and they don't look in mine.

I see several people at the hospital cafeteria who I think won't make it. I see a person so skinny I am unsure how she is walking. Many can't walk. The doctors and the chaplain tell me again: commit to your treatment.

I search for stories, accounts, and reckonings of this experience from the perspective of outsiders from the dominant story of how this all goes. I look again for stories of going through this told by women, queers, people of color, immigrants, poor people, by parents. I find some. Not a lot. I must remember what I wrote before, since I forget a lot these days. I have had this or that experience before and forgotten it. But, this time, deeper and further in treatment, my theories about why these books don't exist are different—more emotional, less coherent. I still think it is probably because many potential authors simply die. But then I also think that some of them probably give up and feel ashamed of giving up. Or maybe they finish treatment and still are ashamed of surviving so fundamentally changed, or they have the desire to forget treatment, and crawl back into the healthy world quickly.

Those crawling through cancer today, in this time of un-making, might be too damn tired or overwhelmed to write it down, render it, or expose it—this deep wound of poisoning and what it reduces one to. "I am diminished, diminished," I think. Others must feel that too. It makes me want to write more, write louder, write messier. I am not ashamed; I have vastly less to lose. I want many others to realize they have less to lose, too. I am not unique, just loud and unrelenting in my desire to feel less alone.

This poison is aggressively intimate. I taste it in my mouth for days, as if holding poisoned bark between my teeth hour after hour. It makes me radioactive for two full days after infusions. The chemotherapy is so hazardous that it makes my body unsafe for my loved ones to be around. No one in my household can do my laundry or touch my urine, tears, vaginal fluids, vomit, or blood. I clean my toilet twenty times a day to not poison my family. The poison provokes a pain in my bones that starts at the very root of where they took shape in my mother's womb. It feels like an original wound, an ancestral one. It forces me up to walk endlessly around the block and then back to bed, with whatever pain relief I can find. It pushes me beyond functioning, beyond assumptions, beyond all I thought I knew. My menopause meets that pain, oddly and brutally. I lie in bed hot, then cold, enraged, then sorrow-logged.

An injection patch on my arm for bone marrow growth aches and flashes its green light again and again in the dark, making me wonder if my bedroom is an airport. Am I the plane or the landing strip?

• • •

My body is smooth, like a 1970s commercial for Nair. Only the sparse, blond hair right above my knees survives. This body is filled with her own eccentricities. It is usually above 100 degrees in the summer in Phoenix. Every time the sun hits my small, bald head, I feel a metallic sweat covering my body like I'm exuding hot tin. When I lick my lips, it tastes slightly of poisoned sap. I say to the yew tree's poison: ah, the sun touches you and you want to come out of me and go back to it. As I burn, I like to look at the hot, slate-colored mountains, and remember that there are secrets, tiny amounts of water buried within and beneath them.

Committing, getting up and going to treatment again is the main thing I build hours and days around. And though I have had real pain in my life, I realize that I live in a dominant and dominating culture that taught me very little about the ability to commit to something very painful and long-term. The symbolic martyrdom of social justice work is often short-term—all of it far less painful, in my experience, than this. Perhaps "pain" should be split into multiple words because added adjectives don't cut it. "Excruciating pain," for example, just doesn't cut it. Maybe three different English words would be better. Is there such a thing as soul pain, body pain, or energy pain? Existential pain? Because I have felt like I wanted to give up before, but it was in response to one or two of those other forms of pain. Now I face a pain I know no words for, me, who loves words so desperately. And in her face, I realize I never knew her before: she is a wig snatcher, she is a soul flattener, she is a ruthless humbler of all she meets, she is a boundary in and of herself. Yet, in her face, all creatures know who and what we are and our limits, and our limits are staggering.

I pray:

Poison yew, come into all parts of me. I know you have come to kill both that which is killing me and that which protects my body. I know you are here to kill the sick and the healthy. I know you move and vanquish in a place where good and bad don't exist. I know I will never be the same after my cancer and after you. I know your healing power is that of a killer. So, I offer you my cancer cells to kill; I offer you my white blood cells to kill, I offer you my bone marrow to eat. As you run through every tributary of my body, I choose you. Come into me, killer. Remake me. Set me free.

Come into us all, killer. Burn away the dominators and their enablers, their stories; burn away our poor, limited, and broken imaginations; burn away what we thought was good or bad. We have no fucking idea. Let us find out what comes after this. Let us build not from ruins we critique, but from fresh ash that has completely cleared the ground. Come into us, killer. Remake us. Set us free.

• • •

There has never been a period of my life so sharply governed by a cycle. From birth to death, we are part of many cycles inside the larger one. Moon cycles. Life cycles. Cycles of emotion that always change. Cycles of conjuring: all we bring to life changes and dies. Though a worldview of domination and violence has brought us to the brink of species death or transformation, an extinction cycle of all life forms is not only normal but also always inevitable. A species so intensely narcissistic finds this a difficult reality.

Zombie life is one way of thinking about beings who try to exist outside of cycles. No wonder they fascinate humans living in a late-stage capitalist culture of unharnessed greed, violence, lies, and subjugation. We feel disgusted by how different zombies are from us; I think now, we're disgusted at how similar we are to them. The dead eyes, the flesh-eating, the empty shuffle. The cliché of one endless artificial run on our treadmills in front of our screens. Alive on a planet of dying oceans and endless fire, where, as Audre Lorde warned, everywhere we look (or choose not to look) is the congealed blood of the dead. Those who rule are so deranged and arrogant that they force their death wish on everyone.

Living in submission to natural cycles is my way to come back to life after wasting so much time in my personal story, my own zombie shuffle. As a young person, I yielded to these cycles with much more ease and wonder; I remember being that young, queer, white hippie in college who would sit on moss in the woods and bleed into the earth. I was so clear about the seasons, the cycles, and the joy of passing into older and older age.

At some point, I lost this skill, this joy—otherwise, I would have seen the signs my body was giving me, the many signs. Those signs had to do with cycles, and I ignored them. I had painful periods for years, but I was always catching a plane to go to work, to save the world, bleeding through my clothes in some airplane bathroom—too many meetings, campaigns, and trips to go to a doctor to find out what was wrong. I was irregular in my cycle for fifteen years and I always blamed it on travel. There was little I wouldn't sacrifice for my work and the political causes behind and beneath it. I thought I was changing the world, which meant more to me than my body, sanity, and soul.

This also meant that those around me had to sacrifice and submit to my cycle of urgency—and it was a narrow one. Social change work also has seasons and its own organic work cycles. The art of organizing, uniting people to fight, is the art of grandmothers, first and foremost. When I picture the archetype of an organizer, I picture a grandmother in a housing tenement. I picture how she cares for the residents, the community as a whole, and unites them for the best outcome for everyone while taking no bullshit. Like most things, this sacred art has been poisoned by greed, money, and power. What that means now is that even our organizing shops that say they stand for justice are not built in the image of the grandmother. They are primarily fueled by cowboys and bosses who have arranged their lives in solitary ways, or they have subordinates or spouses/family members to take care of all aspects of life so that they can impose that impossible work cycle on the rest of us. I assume even the organizing cowboys mean well; they just stopped listening. These cycles, impossible to sustain, take us further and further away from the molten bone marrow of this planet, which is *organically* cyclical; it is sustainable by design. Sustainable in a way we are far too puny to understand. The wisdom in ecological design promotes immunity and is created by powers far greater than us. These are the cycles I want to submit myself to, to let change me, make me over.

Cycles take us by force. One way or another, one day or another, they will come for us. Growth is organic and often destructive. It takes force to move matter, to move beings from old shapes into new ones. A cycle came for me. The kind of cycle that grabs a person by the spinal column and says, "I dare you, on your knees, to say that life moves in a straight line, a one-way trajectory."

In my life cycle now, a yew tree poisons me to the point of bone break, then I get high on steroids for three days, up at 4 a.m. cleaning the house, so that my body won't reject its medicines. Then I spend four days in agony that makes a time of no pain impossible to recall. During it, it seems I have never been without pain, and I never will be again. Then I spend ten days weak, buzzing, and ringing, but mostly functional. Then it starts again.

Fentanyl to OxyContin to Taxol to Carboplatin to Benadryl to Dexazone to marijuana to Ondansetron.

Walnuts to watermelon to avocado to turkey tail to reishi to cranberries to yams.

Tears to talk to altar to silence to TV to reading to altar to reading to tears to altar to silence.

I have never lived through a cycle as intense as I am surviving now. But I will never again believe that anything I live through is not a cycle. Awake at last, I promise myself that for as long as I have left, I will never walk on the timeless, heartless, dull, and vacant road again.

● ● ●

I lie in my bed while my mother cuts up a pineapple in the kitchen, my bed-hog three-year-old snoring by my side. I told a friend last week that there should be two words to distinguish what my mother is now doing for me—it is so extraordinary—and the bare minimum of what a mother might do.

My mother, responsible for many other family members in her own home and life—including two other young grandsons who miss her a great deal—stopped her life to move to Arizona and help me save mine. She has an immune-system disease that makes dryness and heat painful to her. There is little in Arizona besides dryness and heat in the summer. When the only thing I can eat is a tuna fish sandwich, and only then if it can be made in three minutes flat, she makes it. She washes the car, gets groceries, plays endlessly with a tantrum-throwing three-year-old, and watches shows that only an incredibly high cancer patient would want to watch on TV. She does all this for her wayward, wayfaring daughter.

I have not lived consistently at home since I was fifteen. Whole sections of my life have been obsessively arranged around my work. I have skipped visits home to vacation with a lover or partner. Despite such neglect, I have still been demanding. I call her and I monologue. By a cookie-cutter white standard, I have been an okay daughter. By the high standard she sets by example, from culture, from being an immigrant, and from her own spirit, I have not. She knows this, even if she denies it. But here is the interesting thing: she does not care at all. Not now. I am not saying she is a martyr. Not by a long shot. She shows up at 7 a.m. expecting that I have made her coffee the way she likes it, mentioning that no one else in the family seems to be able to pull off coffee the way she likes it, the way coffee is served back home, dark like thick walnut sludge. She expects me to have dinner with her or make a dinner plan for her every night. Her actions say: *I have stepped into a place of love beyond space and time for you, but you will respect me for this.*

The saddest part is that, at first, she thought I didn't want her to come. That is the part I have never been able to write in this book without weeping: to admit how good I am at not knowing how to name what I need, how skilled at pushing people away. When she first arrived, there were weeks when I raged and vented. I told her I had thought I would die, and she had not been there. She looked at me and said, "But you told me not to come. It was COVID. And you were so good at listing all the reasons I shouldn't. You are an adult. I cannot read your mind." She was right. And I am lucky she came anyway.

Mothering is a verb. I remember a conversation with a dear friend, holding his hand while he sobbed and worried over his two teenage girls, saying, "But they don't have a mother." Without a second thought, I said: "Of course they do. You are their mother." I had seen him doing that work so many times: staying in it with your kid when no one else wants to, when it is brutal and when it is boring—holding them, rooting for them, bearing them, shaping them, and constructing space for them to be shaped by others.

Mothering when you are losing (or have temporarily lost) your ability to mother in the ways you wish is something different. All the tiny actions you want to execute that you cannot. Some days you are enraged at the simple cavalier details of what others can do with their children, what your co-parent can do with your child, what your own mother can do with your child. You feel rage at how easily they name these details, like taking your child on trips, when you feel you will never be able to do such things again. Other days you long to hear these sweet details, fantasizing that you, too, could participate. When you are functional and lucky enough to have him with you, even as you can barely care for him, you close your weak fist around his little hand for an hour as he sleeps.

These are the urges that help me understand this long, unusual, and frankly amazing time with my own mother. I am thirty-nine years old; I was raised to be quite independent. Her presence for several months is a far cry from mere phone calls and holidays together. Day after day, I see in her eyes the same thing I feel for my child: unrelenting, furious, and unstoppable love. Her face says, "You are of me, and I will drag you back to life whether you like it or not, want it or not, think you need me or not." I hope to be half the mother she is.

CHAPTER 5

Zombie Life, Summer 2021

I am sitting in a restaurant, and a man at the bar is wearing a t-shirt that says, "Pain is weakness leaving your body." I want to walk up to him with the sharp knife next to my plate and stab him. Only if you have never known pain as your closest companion, your most intimate presence, could you wear a shirt like that. Only if you are so lost that you must constantly see yourself *in competition with pain*. I am angry because there has been so much pain around me, and I have not shown up for others in pain. I have not seen their pain; I have made excuses for my discomfort with their pain. This fills me with shame.

Physical pain forces us into our bodies—and we see how others look at us. The shock of seeing someone bald for the first time, the bald of a newborn, the feathered snowy aura. I see it in the mirror. I also see it through the eyes of others.

When people see me on the street now, they look away. Or they can't stop looking. I can't change that. So, I am trying not to look away from myself. I am trying to ask those who love me not to look away. I feel ashamed to say how often I *have* looked away, without meaning to, from those in my life who are suffering deeply. Those who, for a long or short time, are not *able*, in various ways, to do a variety of things. I have been impatient. I have also been staunchly and intensely present and then simply *gone*. I think about how these patterns have impacted my relationships. I think about how many I have known who were sick and I didn't reach out to.

At the same time, I think the world owes me nothing, and, if I am honest, I would only show up with intensity and daily tenacity for my own closest people. It makes sense that this is who is showing up for me. We forget the simple fact that the world revolves around no one. It already has its own rotation, its own sun.

Yet, I remember the simple acts of others so clearly through my haze of drugs—a card, a text, a visit, bad jokes, weekly flowers. Many show me they care about me, and it matters deeply.

I am truly fortunate that those closest to me do not form a small circle, every day I try to show the truth to them a bit more—the messy, erratic truth. I am on so many different medications and handling radical and sudden menopause. So my moods and perceptions are up and down. That is not always easy for people to meet. Some meet it with compassion, for others, it is a reason to continue to be angry at me when they were already. It is not easy to show up for. My cottage, shades drawn, looks like the person it houses: my son is gone, and its sole occupant is like a shadow with its eyes closed.

•••

After almost a year of blood draws, IVs, and now poisoning, my veins are scarred, swollen, and fragile. Nurses must use an ultrasound machine to find one that won't reject their painful penetration. I feel like they are whale watching in the sea of my body. Waiting for a sonar echo. At the end of chemotherapy, the saltwater flush after the chemo drip felt like the sea burning its way into the waterways of my body. My blood pushes back against the pain, sending a bright red tendril into the IV drip. I look at it: my plasma fighting back into the sea via my exhausted vein. The nurse calmly holds a heat pack to my arm: it is only the vein spasming, she says, your veins are shutting down.

I think of my veins as animate for a second. They've had enough of being pierced, penetrated, taken from, and forced to take in poison. Not unlike how being a woman has felt for me at many points in my life; not unlike how the rest of my body feels right now. These days, I don't self-advocate. I won't say I have had enough. I don't say anything. I just sit in my chemo recliner and cry tears over my yellow tissue paper mask until it looks like the wrapping on a birthday present that got left in the rain. My loved ones look on quietly and sadly. I don't want to be touched. Sometimes I can't be touched; it hurts too much.

But crying helps. Now I let myself cry whenever I want or need to. I don't care how many nurses see; I don't care that the patients around me are old, white men, suffering but not able to cry or smile near me. They have the same bird-shaped heads, the same tubes sticking out of them as they walk to the bathroom. For the first time, I do look into their eyes, even if they can't meet mine. Never one to cry in public, I know why I do now: I submit to the function of tears as I do to any part of my body that still works.

• • •

On a good night, I lie on the shitty cot I must put beside my son's bed to cuddle, because my bones are too brittle and my skin too weak for him to sleep in my bed. Before you feel too sorry for me, you should also know that I love cuddling him but have hated sleeping in bed with him for years because I would get up two or three times a night before I had cancer, and he is a brute of a bed companion, like most small children. On this night, he has fallen asleep with the back of his head digging into my ribs. My right hand is on his warm, exposed belly. He finally dozed off after staring at the ceiling and muttering about stars and bells. I think again that pain has diminished me, muted me; it has humbled me, at times nearly broken me. It has done the same to many, bringing us almost to death so that we may live. But it has not permanently reduced me. I am not smaller; I am not less. I am not permanently diminished.

Oh, to be angry and have cancer and be a woman living outside the lines in a time of zombies. Not grateful, not agreeable, not sad. But, filled with rage in a world where my insurance company has deemed my bone marrow injections medically unnecessary, I am reduced to sobbing to their customer service representative, saying, "You work your whole life, and this is all you get. My bones will break apart if I go forward with chemo without these injections. I have no bone marrow, don't you understand? Please. Please. I can't afford $14,000 for each shot."

Rage and sadness at the moments when even people I deeply love simply cannot show up for my survival, having no idea how to put anyone first but themselves. Most of us seem to be caught in a binary of extremes; unable to put anyone else before ourselves or unable to ever put ourselves first. We yearn profoundly for wholeness, yet that which would bring balance evades us again and again. We seek help from others, but it remains out of reach. Even tectonic plates of the earth know when to move. Most creatures know when to lead and when to follow. Yet, we languish, swinging back and forth in the chasm of self-obsession and self-hatred. A way forward will require courage, tenacity, and fortitude. Where can we find the will and the grace? Tonight, I am the last person with such answers. *I hope only to be fortified in the great change of seasons through which we all must live. I hope to find not peace but power in the life force that moves among us, unleashed and unleashable.*

• • •

After the next chemo round, my steroids have me up again at 4 a.m. each morning. By 7 a.m. Phoenix temperatures are on their way to 118 for the day, so I use the time I have while it is still dark. "Tired and wired," I think to myself and smile. It is what I used to say at morning check-ins at gatherings or when leading a campaign at work. After many long days, that's how I would say I felt. I had no idea at the time that the outer limits of feeling could unite those two words. Brake and gas. Brake and gas. There is only one way to drive a car like that: Steer away from crashes and ride the bucking out. I time my wide-eyed mania so that I can go out into the morning desert with peaches and pecans, see the sun come over the mountains, make an offering with my hands in the sharp rock desert dirt. I have never been as grateful as I am for the days of the month when I can drive.

• • •

I allow myself to think seriously about the possibility of living twenty more years. With many cancers, doctors never tell you about your chances in more than five-year incre-ments. But, if your five-year chances look good, the next five could as well. Twenty more years, I would be fifty-nine. It sounds so luxurious from where I sit in my dark green bed. "I'll take it. I'll take it," I grunt to myself before I fall back into bed, into the slow not-caring of opioids.

• • •

I find our time to be one of profound reckoning—and the possibility (but not promise) of profound realization. Legions of ordinary human beings have been willing to tell the truth about our lives and our ancestors' lives in ways that have not been amplified, multiplied, and shared at such a scale before. Those of us who have been pushed to the margins and silenced, who don't win the domination rat race, are giving the gift of voice and consciousness to the wider world. We dare to whisper, name, summon, and shout what generations before us have told us to keep quiet about, for safety or submission. We speak shakily at first, make art hesitantly, but when we realize we are in good company, with more assurance.

We are hearing the voices of women, people of color, people with disabilities, LGBTQ people, and voices from all around the world. And we are hearing from places we never have before. The use and abuse of oppressed peoples are not in any way new. What is new is the access and resources we have to name the legacies of domination and surveillance, of harm so ancient and durable that it is hard to see paths beyond it. Sorrow, loss, and grief are given voice and the oxygen they should have had hundreds of years ago. This voice comes forth from the mouths of millions and floods the land. It floods and waters the earth. The soil smells of rot and decay for some time. And then, new things, unseen when the earth was too dry, begin to grow.

Thus, we arrive at a time that summons builders, makers, and generators past and present to come forward. So many in the spirit world are rooting for the drowning of bullies, narcissists, and blowhards. But realignment with cyclical life means understanding that our time cannot only be about the downfall of enemies; it must be about the rise of creators.

"Good enough leadership" has overturned my understanding of what "doing our part" now means. The old definitions no longer fit our time. I don't reject the concept of leadership. Instead, I feel a steady pull towards a different set of meanings that define those leading us forward and showing us the ways—words like *creators, collaborators, conjurers*, and *conveners*. I use words like *nurturers, generators, builders, counselors*. I see the life force of words like these all around me in human beings playing different roles: librarians, teachers, organizers, writers, artists, elected officials, cooks, local business owners, environmental engineers, nurses, and childcare providers. We have arrived at a time with new needs, new structures, and we can bring new and renewed energy to what we build. We can be open to how we begin to do the work of now anew.

We can make the social and political world anew and make it in the image of what will never be new: the earth herself, the wild itself, the oldest and most beautiful design. We can mimic her patterns, cycles, and designs. We can uplift beings and elements who have never betrayed these patterns and designs. We can do this for ourselves, and we can do this for her, in homage to the time we still have left being in and of her as a species. It will mean a radical reimagining and surrendering to our vision—what we dare to hope for, how we understand collaboration, how we re-understand power, even how we understand ourselves as individuals, and what it means to be one and what it means to be many. The harbinger of death is no excuse. Fear is no excuse. They will come whether we are different or not, in motion or not. At least, if we take the risk to change, they will come for us when we are not stiff, rigid, locked, but flexing and flexible, perishable, believing, mid-attempt.

As a young person, I read Ursula K. Le Guin's novels. In one world she creates, there are different kinds of magicians who lead and teach. They have titles: Master Namer, Master Summoner, Master Patterner, and Master Doorkeeper. I have long thought titles like this much more useful for understanding the work that happens between people, our skills and abilities, like the work of reading a room or a group, the work of repairing harm, the work of holding space for groups to struggle and make decisions and be in motion. The work of summoning spirit power into groups, quieting groups, fortifying groups. What do we name? What do we summon? What do we pattern? Who keeps the doors, the thresholds between spaces? In the end, it is not us alone but the relationships that impact us. It is not occurrences but their contexts that matter.

•••

Necrosis is defined as the localized death of a living tissue. I think again about what happens when a part of us dies and the rest lives on. Since the spring, when parts of my body were returned to the earth, I have felt compelled to think about this. Dissection is the process of taking apart and trying to understand what is already dead. The idea is that to understand a tree, you kill a tree or wait for it to die and study it. It is an excellent worldview for the impatient, the brutal, the cruel. It is a form of study wholly unlike planting a tree, nurturing a tree, sitting under a tree, or cutting wood from a tree that has died. To kill something to understand it is to not understand it in wholeness. To assume that an understanding of necrotic flesh translates to an understanding of living flesh is fallacy. This deadening framework carries far beyond biology classes. It is the worldview within which we pervert and distort everything we touch: community, culture, and institutions. We live in a time when people are so scared to build that they critique for destruction not construction.

Many old ways of thinking—ideas, infrastructures, and institutions—needed to die. Many of us have set about ripping them apart. This is part of a natural cycle. Yet, it gives our generation few skills in tilling, planting, building, nurturing. We can use critique to build things better. But, when we dissect, we treat human beings and social structures as though they are already dead. We open our skin, poke flesh, and push our organs around with a callousness that neither the dead nor the living deserve. Our collective pain is already immense; so much and so many have already died. Some things need to die, and violence has a natural purpose. It ends old ways of being. It yields much, but not understanding. Character assassination kills something inside the assassinated and the assassin.

To vanquish someone, to shame them for mistakes, to kill their spirit and drive—doesn't save us from uncertainty. It might give a short, sweet burst of righteousness but little else. However much we distance ourselves from the other, the vanquishing will haunt us.

• • •

Cancer is the growth of cells where they shouldn't be, cells that defy limits and cross the boundaries of the tissues around them. I do not feel at war with my illness. Instead, I think about my inability to set boundaries clearly or well throughout my life to date, my inability to be precise— to, for instance, show up clearly and consistently for my ancestors though I marked my body as committed to them as a young woman: my first tattoos being purely religious. I think about many places inside me with the inability to clearly say no, or yes. I think about my relationships, my desire to be close to others, and my attempts to articulate the spaces between us. I think about how hard it has been for me to say what I want in the face of those wants being different from the desires of those I love. It is almost a cliché, a tragic one, how many women require cancer to figure out what we need and do not need, what we want and do not want. Desire for approval and desire to please wane, but what waxes for me is a terrifying groundlessness beyond my allegiances, commitments, and loyalties—what will I do with the rest of my life if I can win it back? If I can find it?

• • •

It is an easy courage, my ability to say things others won't say aloud; easy because death feels so close to me, and others see it around me. I get a time-limited pass. Expiration dates and the specter of loss create particular pressure on relationships. How will these bonds live, die, change? Though I am just one person, shaving her head in the mornings to remove even the one-quarter centimeter of poisoned hair, I commit to my refrain of truth-telling. And, as the truth slowly changes my life, I realize how much before was untruth and obligation. Like all people who are compromised, unable, and in deep need, I am at the mercy of the distance between who I said I was and who I am on any given day. Deep, sharp, and bloody ravines of hypocrisy create a gnawing shame and denial. Ordinary people try to prove we are who we say we are; institutions and international leaders do the same. But often enough we are just not those people in those moments, the people we think we are, the people we say we are. Spiritual and political organizations, designed in the image of a liberatory and transformative future, break our hearts and bodies, and souls the most: the promise and romance are so great, the expectations so high. We don't believe the hype anymore, and neither does anyone else. If we could admit that truth, we could look each other in the eyes.

This does not happen for lack of intent or hard work. It happens because we drink and eat and dream from what is served to us at the toxic table of domination. We conjure what we know to call upon. It is not individual failing; it is collective amnesia and a shitty diet of domination.

● ● ●

When I go to make an offering in the desert again at 4 a.m., on steroids again, I spy what was once the center of an ancient, giant tree—I can see its many rings as it lies there on its side. Now it's still the shape of wood, but has the feeling of stone when I touch it, what science calls petrification. I sit by it. I lift the apple I brought and cut it open through its belly to show its heart (the shape of a pagan star and a Slavic holiday sign for good luck) and touch it to my forehead. I wonder if I've poisoned it with chemo sweat. It has touched my skin: should I still eat my half and offer the other? I chuckle and shrug. What is a little more poison? I look at the stone that was once wood. It does not seem to hate itself so much that it is unwilling to change form. I shrug again, eat my half. It tastes, predictably, like the poison of the yew tree, like biting into a copper bracelet. But I remember how it tastes without metal. And it may taste that way for me again.

I used to think fear was the main factor in why most of us struggle so much to change form. Or why we suffer so much as our form is changed for us. Now I wonder how much is due to our inability to accept what we have done in our current shape. We are unready to leave it behind to become something new and probably, for a while, uncomfortable. Yet the earth is already being changed by us and changing everything for us. Deep, deep down we know our descendants will change form: look, smell, and be different than us, even if we are not ready ourselves.

But some of us are ready. Some of us are aching to change. Like me, they have hit rock bottom. I remember that day— my veins spitting red back into my IVs. "Returning blood" is what the nurses call it. I like the way it sounds—like it is a good thing: my blood overflowing its plastic waterway, pushing through the tubes, to meet the poison. My blood says: we have had enough for today. We can change some more tomorrow.

•••

The doctors explain that I am simply in one of the highest percentiles for pain during the treatment they are administering because of dosage and my age. They shrug: nothing personal. I, meanwhile, spend two whole cycles of hell trying to get medicated properly. Finally, by round three, I meet my goal: lying in bed while my knees, thighs, and ankles buzz like great oaks being cut down by chainsaws, but I feel nothing. In *The Body in Pain*, Elaine Scarry talks about the idea of torture as an unmaking of one's world and of chemotherapy as a form of torture.

Perhaps this is why I feel the urge to record my perspective not only of my own illness but of everything in my entire world during this time: the unmaking of one's world is brutal and reducing, but also has bright liberatory moments. More and more, I look at others and instead of thinking *I am afraid*, I think, *we are all wasting time.*

CHAPTER 6

Change That Cannot Be Undone, Summer, 2021

I cannot tell you I wrote a great deal in these pages during the middle of my treatment, as my physical and mental health worsened. I can tell you what happened instead. People here in Phoenix who love me stayed and continued to care for me day after day after day. My partner loved me and did a million small and big things for me, too many to count. My blood family stayed ever present, in person or on the phone. People who loved me from afar got on planes, risking their own health, and came to me in the dead of a painful summer of heat. They mopped the floor, they made soup or other mild food, they cleaned out the fridge, they helped me walk when I could not. They told me stories about all we had been together in the past, reminded me of who I was, who I didn't have to be anymore, and their hopes and love for the new/old person who would return from this.

They took me to gay bar patios when I could go, or taco shops. Sometimes, we talked about the world's spiritual, political, and ecological future. I would do my best, even though my mind would often not find words or follow clear paths in the conversation. It would last a few brief moments, on my worst days, and then they would help carry me back to the car. They loved me in the quiet of an intimacy unrecorded, undocumented, where no one watched from afar, or on a screen, and I allowed myself to let guard after guard down and be loved like never before. I learned to say when I could not talk, walk, or function, and answer questions about needs even when I couldn't ask.

My pain increased. My symptoms increased. As I got halfway through my treatment, my veins began to give out, and, to get through it, I had to lie in bed and think of other arteries in me, taking in different substances than only poison. I pictured the different spirits of those around me pushing love into my riverways, giving me different medicines. With their own bitter, queer, scrappy stories and care, with their own fears for their own health, with their elixirs of dirty jokes, with all our shared history binding us, with their passion to keep living when it was hard for them to do so, as it was for me. In this way, I lived my days, and we lived our days. It was imperfect. Some circumstances made me angry. I tried to keep the relationships that were not functioning out of my daily sphere because I couldn't bring much good to those.

There was no sewing me back together then. I was a river shining with chemicals. I had to come apart.

•••

I have spent some time lying in my shiny, gray sheets debating if it is principled to use the phrase "the rape of veins." Throughout my life, with the exception of moments of radical claiming of my own experience, I have been a day-to-day "underplayer." Like so many women I know from all walks of life. We underplay the efforts we make to partner, we mother, work hard, get by with too little sleep, buffer others from feelings, mediate conflict, do the hard thing; getting by, an "it's not so bad" person.

I have not been the white woman who cries in public, in groups, have not used tears for manipulation. But there is a point in intravenous cancer treatment where one's veins start to give out. They don't need to rest anymore; it is beyond that. They are tubes ribboned in scars and can no longer be cut into in the same place again. No other phrase in the English language could describe this feeling but "the rape of veins." Now the nurses say: "Think of crying like blowing your nose during this procedure. You need to do it. It clears you out to let it out."

Sometimes in the morning, I spend twenty minutes trying to restart my approach to the day. I have been up every hour on the hour throughout the night with hot flashes and then pain in my hands and feet. I lie there and wait with my eyes closed until I can greet the day differently, with less hopelessness and resentment.

Yes, torture is still unmaking my world, it is not done yet. Consciousness digs a tunnel and forces me through into the dark, where roots and soil dwellers come at me daily. Once I was on a balcony, living life on the deck of a great ship, now I am below deck all the time. Torture separates me from most people that I know my age. The counselors ask me if I know anyone else with cancer, and I say well yes, two friends. But then I remember, though they were the only two people I know who have been through the same kind of torture before age forty, there are only certain times any of us want to talk about it. Our bodies buck the inauthenticity of making metaphors or tolerating lazy and false comparisons.

●●●

As a younger person, I never read biographies. This year, I saved special brain space to read three quite long ones: Adrienne Rich, Audre Lorde, James Baldwin. I felt their contexts and thought about their difficult lives and choices like never before. I suppose I suddenly cared much more about the specificity of how they lived and, particularly, how they suffered.

My world is slowly, daily, unmade, unraveled. Cut apart. My choices stripped from me methodically, fewer and fewer each day. After the shock and the shame—that I have been able-bodied my whole life in a way that led me to mistreat my body, mind, and soul (thinking always "she can take it," as though I were speaking of someone other than myself). I also come back to the realization that came to me after surgery—that I never actually understood anything about disability, about what it means to be completely unable to do so many things. To walk, to talk, to remember what day it is, to drive, to go to the bathroom on my own.

I never really understood the visceral difference between needs and wants, something many others know. Then I joined the odd ranks of the temporarily disabled: proven, in no small part, by the short-term disability check I get in my tiny, hot, metal mailbox. It speaks to the power of ableism, that this revelation (again it fills me with shame to say) balloons me with desperate longing to be healthy and able again.

In brief moments or days of sobriety, I am overcome with specific desires: for my eyebrows to grow again, to see dark, ruddy peach fuzz on my bald head—signaling life—to be able to walk without the support of hands or furniture, to feel well and fully my fingers and feet. I await the autumn, knowing my body will never be the same, but also knowing my integrity will never allow me to unremember and unknow what I now know.

Yet, I am not arrogant, only astonished to keep looking in the eyes of death and feel no fear, to fear only pain. I wish I could tell you that, in that time of treatment, old grief and grievances depart: mine did not. The world often tells us we are mandated to feel afraid in such circumstances, to worry without ceasing, leaving little space for curiosity about how someone like me really feels. There are emotions harder for me than fear, and they came.

How do you let go and allow the unmaking of a life still heavy with joy and sorrow, with ordinary pains and shames, but not filled with fear? Perhaps, this ordeal only showed me that I wasn't that afraid before. It also isolates me from those whose lives are ruled by fear: they don't believe me or have much space for what I do feel.

•••

At first, there was darkness. At the end, darkness. As we pass each threshold, darkness.

One night, as my son falls asleep, this time on my face, staring up into the darkness, he says to me "sharing with you." Sharing this glowing darkness.

Perhaps all the souls longing to be liberated in this world, those of us with the courage to dream of an utter and raw liberation, an undoing of domination, come to dwell in the warmest, earthiest darkness. We will not be alone there. Those who emerge from the water ready for this specific time, are not afraid of darkness.

•••

As I've said, the possibility of making a life anew has been brought to me by the people who, week after week, knit me back together. I called them back to me, across space and time. They came, reminded me of times I had been there for them, that we had been together in all the big ways that make the most highlighted memories in a life. I summoned them without knowing it. They reminded me of who I once was, and who I am. I was sometimes surprised to see how much they loved me, to hear what our times together on this earth have meant to them. They flew across the country in COVID to be with me, they brought their children, they ran errands, bought out IKEA, cooked salmon dinners, and gossiped with me. They helped me walk.

I have always been very bad at marathons. I am a sprinter, often impulsive and in the moment. So, I needed long haulers, people around me who are good with patience and steadiness, to see me through. Sometimes, day-to-day life in Phoenix was filled with my closest people like that—I stopped questioning how I had come to deserve their love. I did not. It was not a question of deserving: it was grace. They would remind me each day to make the choices that I can still make: cherries or nectarines, gay bar for two hours or trashy movie, drugs or fewer drugs. I remembered again—forgot and then remembered again, grew confused and then remembered yet again—it is physically impossible to see the end of pain when you are in some of the worst medically induced pain possible. Best to stop trying to see the end. Don't concentrate on trying to find the end. Others must help you see how this part ends. That it can. That it will. That there will be something that happens next: anything but this.

•••

As the monsoon season starts in Arizona, I exist in the daily reality of the last six weeks of my treatment: fragile, weak, with skin so barren of hair that it usually hurts when others touch me. I started this journey relieved when my hair fell out because it felt most genuine for the inside of me to match the outside. Now, as my illness and pain have consumed most of this year, I am worn down. I have nothing inspirational to say. I am not committed to my treatment anymore, I am committed to my son, to living, to the hope that I will come through this and feel like living again, like I am more than half alive again. I still commit to this writing, to my stubborn intention to set it all down honestly—to tell the truth here, as I felt it, not *thought* it cerebrally—because the chronicling of this journey is so rare. I try to remember. I try to remember why I am doing any of this at all. The drugs plus the heat of the desert summer put me into a profound stupor. I am isolated by being rarely able to talk, and when I do talk, I can rarely remember the words I want to use.

I cover my head because I just don't want to look at my baldness anymore. When I am well enough to think, I stare at all the women in Phoenix with saline breasts, tucked tummies, and big swollen lips. I think that I know now what it is to want to look different than I do. I wonder, do the bags inside their breasts ache at night? Do their scars hurt? Do their lips sting? Do they wish they still looked like themselves instead of like so many other women in Scottsdale? Maybe they do, maybe they do not. I know I tire of standing out, so bald, shiny, and sick. I want to transform back. Or transform through.

My son asks constantly about the weather because I told him my hair would start growing back when the weather turns cooler again. I hope I am telling him the truth. My choices are limited daily. Pain, confusion, heavy drug use, and isolation erect different walls around my experience. I reflect on how cavalier I was about all the little and large and looming choices I previously made each day. I chose to stop using the anti-nausea drugs and instead try to stabilize the ongoing metallic taste and smell with food: yucca soup, pecans, black cherries, and magenta borscht instead of Zofran. I burn candles every day and open myself to the complicated ancestral dialogue that is the main kind of spiritual support available to me. Not a woman born to easy or calm deities, the conversations have mixed results. My ancestors tell me there is no way but the hard way, there is no way but through, every day, their eyes are hidden from me by their head scarves. I can see their hands, but they are in shadow.

I continue to welcome those close to me, week after week, still taking turns and braving planes and 108 degree weather to walk with me through this journey, reminding me to pay rent and take pills, but also reminding me again (since I have forgotten) that I have had a long-roaded, hard-lived life, and that a life that is both new and old waits for me at the end of this burning summer.

But I also feel the need to talk about what remakes my world, or perhaps, what makes it anew.

I live in gratitude of being born queer in this lifetime toward the end of the last century (1981): a state of being, that for me, increased my ability to see not only gender, but the whole damn world as nonbinary, never boring, never benign. The way I learned and lived my queerness not only embedded relationships in a deep, dark thickness; it also brought a cast of characters into my life so intense, so bright that, even when I cannot walk, I sit on my couch, and they dazzle me. In queerness, I can go back in pain each week to the always imperfect touchstones and watering holes of our lives—afternoons with gay-bar barbacks in cowboy hats and cut-off shorts, never staring at me when I can't walk and can barely talk. They have seen it all. The porous, queer friendships—years of staying in love, but falling in and out of contact, only to show up with fresh jokes and news and gossip when I need each of them most.

Even the way they make the schedule itself, so queer, taking turns coming week after week from all over the country. The staff at my gym staring at me calmly, as week after week I sign up yet a different companion to walk slowly with me on a treadmill, holding my hand.

A beautiful, queer, middle-aged couple own the outdoor café. They bring me different unsweetened iced teas to try, hoping one won't make me chemo-sick. I show up on steroids right at 6 a.m. when they open, because I have been up since four.

I started this memoir, reflecting on the directness of my own near-death experience, alongside the more diffuse collective near-death experience of everyone living through a contagious plague—within many other spiritual, cultural, and political contagious plagues: plagues inside plagues. I continue it now as I, of necessity, force myself to look toward future-building. As we reach and surpass our limit of living isolated from each other, I find our language and our stories are inadequate to explain where we have come from, what we have been through, and how we see the future. We are like a huge party where thousands bled to death on the floor, but we are all going back to our previous discussions. The healthy and living, once again sure of their life and its span, struggle to name the gnawing feelings that keep them awake at night. Yet, even the limited stories we hear give us indicators: many or most of us can't sleep; feel great, daunting sadness; lackluster joy in life; and lack the basic necessities to thrive. Some of us are not at all sure we still want to be here, in this time and are voting with our feet, ending our own lives, by one method or another.

I personally am finally sure I want to be here, in this body, in this time, perhaps because I now know what I am willing to do to be here. My life was breathtakingly easier before my illness, but I had much more ambivalence about it than I do now. I (like most cancer patients) also view this exchange very practically: this season of torture in exchange for five, ten, or fifteen more years. However, I do start to feel deeply ambivalent about returning to the person I was, and my previous ways of being. For one thing, I seem to have slowly (at least for the moment) lost most skills of diplomacy, burned away by a downright obsessive desire to be genuine and radically transparent. Lies (my own and others) keep me up at night, while I burn through hot flashes. I sometimes wake up sweaty, angry, bitter, but also often quite clear.

Perhaps it is my own deep, gnawing desire to see a need for myself in the world, a vision like a growling Slavic bear goddess in the night—bejeweled, vain, and hairy. Yet also I see the response all around me to leadership (in any realm or sector of life) that brings authenticity. I see the heads of others turn towards those willing to tell the truth in our time: not falsify or sugar up the realities we now face. An appetite for charm and celebrity lessens, and a new hunger grows for ordinary, daily truths. Perhaps I see it, perhaps I just hope to. Perhaps I also hope so hard for it, that I wish to conjure it, see it grow. My truth is that I have longed for this moment: a moment when celebrity and vanity are less worshipped and realness can get a word in edgewise in US culture. I see that foothold, just an old, simple shoe, one foot holding that door open to the culture. So I want to do what I can to encourage us to feed it: to say that hunger for something besides McDonald's and sugar and fancy, fake faces is a good hunger: let's invite that hunger in, sit her down at our table, cook something real for her, eat it together, then make more real food, eat it together again, and in that way let that hunger grow.

We can't put hunger on a diet, we can't tell that urge solely what *not* to consume, desire, practice. We cannot only tell it to abstain from what is momentarily delicious, but toxic. We must feed it, we must stock homes and kitchens for the new hunger, we must learn to prepare the raw ingredients of a different diet, and then we must feed the new, fragile hunger small meals many times a day. This is what a new way of eating, enforced by cancer, taught me about what you do with new hungers.

This new hunger can be seen in our eyes. Our eyes say to one another: tell me something I can believe. The hunger prompts us to listen to voices that speak of their own struggles and flaws, broken and scarred hands moving around their faces to enunciate. We find and dust off books by writers who give us the hardest scenarios and contexts to digest: writers who remove any easy binary of good and evil. The hunger leads us to nuance—that sneaky lover who satisfies us both more and less at the same time, who leaves us wanting more—in a good way. We see it is all more complicated, contradictory and thicker than we ever thought possible.

Yet, our stories (stories authored and amplified by those of us who still believe that our whole alive world can be liberated, no matter how late the hour) are still primarily corrective. The direction we give to those who seek to live in radical truth and integrity in these times is to change vocabulary a bit and act friendlier to those dominated and generationally traumatized. The hunger for the unplugged, the raw, the real is not sated by this.

We want to be liked; we don't want to be canceled. Perhaps, in a best-case scenario, we reflect some on what we have done, and what we do in our day-to-day lives. Then, those of us who feel entitled to do so, walk around correcting the behavior of others, as though that is our only job on this planet. What we seem to be quite incapable of doing is to engage *who we come from, who we have been, and who we are being.* Who we are is the current manifestation of who we are, not our destiny, but our current truth. The limits of our story keep us in our time, keep us in a version of the world that is limited by our lack of awareness, and the layers of denial that we often accuse our enemies of. The hunger is not sated even inside ourselves, let alone those ancestors who want truths to finally come out, who want their truths finally spoken, who long for reality after being wallpapered over and pushed down for so long.

"Who do you think we are?" these ancestors ask. Yes, who are our ancestors? We throw their names around often these days. But who are they? What made them the way they were and are? They are not all the same, not even within one individual. How is their collective meeting inside of us contentious and/or harmonious? What were their powers? And their impacts? My ancestors come into any room, arguing with each other, arguing within me. The Polish hate the Germans, the Germans disdain the Polish, the witches don't mind the soldiers, but they don't care for the patriarchs who lost their wealth in wars. They will come around when all are summoned at the same time, but I have learned over time to call some more than others. I don't ask all of them for help. Some want to help me, but they are so sad, besieged by regret, and filled with long-ing, never having recovered from losing their home, from their family being wrenched apart by war, and one large dark, cold sea. One comes for me all the time, strong, quiet, bright, and feral: standing with her hair covered, in the woods, with her housecoat pockets filled with wild mush-rooms, her back straight and strong, her will undomesti-cated. She helps me more than the ones who fawn over me, this daughter, this once child, the first on my maternal line to be born on Western soil.

Some of these ancestors worshipped gods, I fear. Some of them worshipped gods I hate. Some of them summoned power I would rather avoid. I crawl and walk my current journey, resigned to the fact that they are unimpressed with all I thought I was here to do, and instead have forced a complete destruction and reconstruction of my life, my purpose, my contribution. Many of our ancestors had great power. Many used that power for profound cruelty and greed. If we believe that our ancestors move with or through us in any way at all, then pretending such ancestors are benign or weak (or feeling guilty about them) does noth-ing to help us become radically transparent about reconcil-ing past, present, and future. When we deny our power, we misuse and abuse it. When we hoard resources, we abuse them and ourselves. What we call "centering ourselves" is a far too mild way of saying that we feel entitled to power. Entitlement is one of the grandest spiritual deceptions in our time; we struggle with how to engage it, and transform it. Most of my life work has been about encouraging myself and others who feel "naturally" entitled to stop taking up so much space and to inhabit space differently. Another part of my work has been an attempt at respectful and genuine encouragement of those with great talent, great potential contribution, and great spirit to feel more entitled to lead from their places of wellness and humility.

Entitlement is not, at its core, about who can and should be visible, but about who, unconsciously, feels that they/we *own* space, time, attention, etc. Entitlement is an escalating problem when literally no one fucking knows what comes next for life on this planet. No one awake can or should trust those who claim to have all the answers. Those claiming absolute knowledge are not leaders: they don't even offer solutions, really. They are people plagued with profoundly unhelpful and noncollaborative limitations of imagination and character. Such people are not trustworthy in a time where trust is paramount. Such people will seek to correct others but not transform themselves, to uplift assumptions and quick half-truths but not take responsibility for themselves. Such people will use brash and grandiose statements to conceal the basic truth that they lack the awareness, temperament, or curiosity to be a builder in this time.

I remind myself again: the great reckonings of our time do not call us *only* to dissect, critique, and dismantle; they also call us to take the vulnerable risks of creation, generating new life through new stories and conjurings that create lifelines and containers for our actions.

My own entitlement led me, for many years, to feel entitled to happy endings in my story, despite the fact, that I am literally surrounded with people who have never known such outcomes, do not expect them, and are snatching moments of night joy from what they see as the jaws of the next morning's destruction. So many of the people I have known live in the reality that tomorrow is *always* a place where anything can happen. The world is not out to punish us individually, nor does it owe us anything. Perhaps this is why most of the written cancer stories I have encountered fall flat and ring hollow for me. Because the celebrated and amplified cancer stories of the entitled are so often about thinking one is cursed with cancer, or blessed to recover from cancer, in the most narrow and individualistic definitions of those terms. I resonate with neither. Cancer is present, comes with all of what it is, and changes everything in its season and in its path. That is all.

Some of us (more of us than we might think) have a great deal of power (to make changes in our own lives) and access, yet we waste precious time trying to conceal and deny that power, in some perverse and cruel game of pretending we do not have it. As we pretend, we are helpless: all the resources we bring to future-building lie fallow in the dead field of our fear. Everyone I care about wants to "get it right," whatever that means to them. Say the right thing. Do the right thing. Live with all the integrity they can muster at this time. Yet deep down we know in this era of corrective culture, we don't need minor corrections in how we interact.

I am clear: to step into visible leadership in this time, in any arena of life, we must get comfortable with being disliked, disagreed with, or disapproved of. A culture of niceness and lies destroys the possibilities of kindness and integrity. The rampant and biting critique of leadership is often warranted (most of the humans who run our world are tyrants, possessed by the demons of greed, cruelty, and indifference), and, yet, sometimes it is not warranted.

We practice character assassination because others are not perfect. We believe they made a mistake, and we cannot suffer the distance between who they say they are and who we find them to be. They are not on our home team. They don't give us attention, or care about us when we deeply need to feel seen and validated. They may not be easy for us to relate to or empathize with. They challenge us. Perhaps, we want to be them. Often, I think, we see them as unprepared to lead, unworthy of our support. We do not find them trustworthy. I used to feel all these things. Sometimes now, as I dare to believe I might fully rejoin the land of the living, I feel them again. But a deeper knowing eclipses that feeling: none of us are prepared to lead. No one knows what they are doing, no matter our competence or experience. The time we live in carries every wound and scar and harm from our human past forward into the present, a time unlike any in human history. So, how could any of us know exactly what to do or how to do it?

Worse still, none of us are entirely trustworthy at any given time. That has always been true. Now, it is a growing truth because we move through a world where every part of us is being changed on cellular and energetic levels by isolation, loss, and profound transformation. We are changing shape because our world is burning, flooding, connecting, numbing, plaguing, purging, and suffering. We live through the death of species all around us, likely including our own.

Transformation is usually cast as bad or good. A sign of "progress" or not. It is none of those things. It is simply change, change that cannot be undone, change that permanently alters the shapes of us and everything around us.

Trust is also cast as a good thing. To be trustworthy is to be consistent, to be as we have been known to be. We say: "I know her. We can trust her." Of course, the goal of being consistent in our actions in support of the liberation of all beings is profoundly positive to me. Full trust requires each of us to rely on other people's "track records," but these times call for many of us to act in unfamiliar ways. We may move in ways that are not the ways we have been counted on to move. We may change our minds. We may make choices, as we take new risks that we will later see as errors. We may make choices that others see as errors right now, and we may disagree. We may be acting in ways unfamiliar and uncomfortable to those around us, and yet, with deep loyalty to our goals.

CHAPTER 7

Rebirth Not Reform, Summer 2021

I decide every day that I still want to be here. We all do. It is obvious to me because deciding to be here currently causes me pain so white-hot it is hard to talk about. I can't go on as I did before. I intend to and must be, different than I have been. I cannot be trusted to be the person I used to be before I saw the face of my death. I may not know death's name, but that is not important. "Near-death" is good enough. Especially if science gives that sickness, that nearness, a name, a very frightening name. *Cancer* is a word that conjures both the thick shell of the crab and the crab's isolation under that shell.

Cancer is not a word deep in my heart or a part of my identity. It is a state of being to me, a season, a threshold, a transfusion, a shedding, a shape-shifting. It doesn't matter if I use a word other than *cancer* for what is happening to me. It is a mark that bestows some strange authority when spoken. The word *cancer,* the experience of it, gives you cultural and communal permission to change. That works in my favor but also makes me impatient. We shouldn't need the political cover of near death to have the ways we change and grow be accepted. So, I made a deal with myself to move forward with this one life, expecting those around me to change profoundly, as I have changed. To make moves

I may not understand, as I am sure I am now doing in the eyes of others. I work, even to trust intent, when people whose actions I have always trusted are now making moves that seem untrustworthy.

To understand what living with a lack of grace for so long has cost me, I must do this. I must do it to understand how the part of me that has lived inside such an exacting and demanding nature has cut my fingers to the bone even as I cut others. I must try to change.

I now know that intent and impact are not the same. I had parroted this rhetoric for years, but now I know. Yet, the way we name their difference is dualistic and vanquishing. The story goes that, for impact to be the priority, which it should be, intent must cease to be relevant. What a cruel perspective, in a time when trying (with no illusions of certain success) will continue to be so key, so needed. When trying and failing, trying and failing, trying and barely doing, then trying and failing again will be the common cadence of a daily wrestle. Self-aware intent takes so much energy as despair surrounds us, will we even attempt to act on it when we dismiss intent and presence so easily now?

• • •

It is sometime in August 2021. I can no longer count days. I rarely use a phone or a computer. Anything with a screen makes me dizzy. I have lost hold of almost all I hold dear, eyes closed, in the long dark, dark tunnel of pain. I have lost count of all the things that I have lost. I am on my hands and knees in the dark. I think of the images in *The Tombs of Atuan* by Ursula K. Le Guin and try to move through the dark by feeling and memory. I am in a tomb, inherently subterranean. I live in the soil, but not in the soil near the surface. I feel no sun. I sit in the house in the shadow. Like a vampire, I come out at night, famished. Some of them were ashamed of drinking blood; I am ashamed of being so poisoned. I don't want to go in public anymore. I don't want to go to the gay bar. I don't want to listen to others talk. I have watched every TV show that I can possibly follow and find interest in, from every friend-donated streaming service you can imagine. I don't care about the plots anymore, the mysteries, nothing surprises me, because nothing is of interest. I can't remember the time before I was using opioids. I can't remember that clarity, that spark. I can't remember a time before this drugged dullness.

I don't care. Everything I said mattered earlier in these pages—I don't care about anymore.

Many days I forget why I am still willing to do this. In the chemo ward, I am surrounded by people giving up, some who admit it and some who cannot. One woman is clearly starving herself to death between chemo treatments. She is fighting with the nurses about her weight, screeching at them that she is eating when she can't be, there is no way she can be. She doesn't want them to know she has given up, she wants to blame them, she wants it to be their fault, but they know she has given up. The louder she speaks, the more softly they answer.

● ● ●

I drag myself to a healer witch who says, a week before my last chemotherapy treatment, as I lay naked on her table: "One more time swimming in the underworld. One more time for now." She says she sees only ancestors around me now, no living spirits. Every living spirit has left my side, they can't take it, they don't know this place I move in now: the bottom, the bottom of this ocean of pain and apathy.

In the dark of another burning hot day, with the windows all closed, I pray to an altar covered with plants and candles, not for the strength to come back to life, but for the strength to be reborn, for the strength to live into being the person I am coming back as. The breath of the dead fills my small cottage, they have not just been passing through these last few months, they have been living here with me.

I pray for the strength to be the person with the power to be this weak, this raw, and this exposed. I see her when I look in the mirror: the bald head, the tattoos I got when I was cavalier with youth and good health. The ones on my arms that people compliment in public. I want to tell them, with the truth serum/poison in my veins: "I was desperate for meaning and purpose when I got these, for allegiance. Can't you see they were only the blueprint that beckoned this destiny to me? Flowers that look like spiders from afar, all the ink concentrated too much in one place. The flowers are incomplete without both the darkness and the light."

I must believe that, for all of us who have had our wombs taken from us, the insides of our bodies are not an empty space, something else grows there. In the Dark. I say aloud to my God, my Mother: "I have been humbled. I sit on the chalk-ghost ground with my back against the great gates of death, agreeing to the terms of my rebirth. I see my boundaries, my limits. Let me go. Let me come back now. Please. Please. Please."

•••

I talk to myself, unsure if I am dreaming or awake.

I dream awake that we live in a realm of humans, each of whom lives in a completely different dream. Entranced. The dead and dying are all around us, as the fires and the floods rage on and on without ceasing. We burn, and we hide from the burning in dead buildings, made of dead materials, purposing us towards inner deadness. I will tell the truth: for someone as prideful, as stubborn, and as strong a storyteller as me, it took this to change me. I had to go chemo-dreaming into the underworld five times, with one more to go. But I am not alone in swimming among and around the dead, I am not alone in my deep fear of being reborn. It is hard to say, I must shed some pride to do so, but I have had times when I have been more afraid to come back than to die. Pain has worn me down and outlasted me so many times, I surrendered and declared defeat so long ago it is a moot point. The writer and therapist Esther Perel talks about growing up in a community of Holocaust survivors and how clearly she saw that some did not die, and some came back to life, but that these are two different conditions.

Underneath zombie culture, underneath what we call collective loneliness, I feel our fear—fear of our ancestors, fear of each other, fear of life. All our skin is like mine is now: too tender, and painful when touched. We are afraid it will still hurt to be touched. I feel my own fear sober me for a minute from my drug stupor as I sit on my bathroom floor writing this:

> I repeat it again and again in this text, and what I need to remember again and again: we are afraid of being fully alive in this time. We do not know what a life of integrity is in this now, a story we can be part of. Our minds are fooled but our bodies are not. In the spaces where our muscles meet, in the places where we are simply part of one species of this planet, we know that we live in the time when it all changes, in that time of endings beyond comprehension. We live in a time of great death. Nothing and no one we love is permanently spared from this cycle of destruction. It burns, it floods, it kills, and we feel it, even if we cannot access that knowledge. At night, alone in our minds, we are not at all sure if we will be here when death becomes fertile life again. We all know this. Yet, we can still see this part through. We can choose not to look away. We can honor

life with our intention and purpose. We can be broken but steady hands. The person I was before would have followed the last sentence with a rousing speech, on a soapbox. Habits of lifelong activists die hard. I started to write the next soapbox sentence. And then erased it. It wasn't real. Instead, I just leave it in broken, steady hands.

•••

I spent so much of my adult life thinking that loving other women and queer people in the most intimate ways was about helping them chase and feed their dreams and their demons, enabling them. Who I was really enabling was myself. It sounds like martyrdom, except that diagnosis would obscure how that served me in avoiding my own demons. These demons have never made life feel carefree for me, and I have let them take so much peace and joy from me. I have started to say goodbye to them now, sadly. They are the demons of the old shape, and I am quite terrified to see the demons of the new person I will be. Though, perhaps that is the best we can wish for sometimes: new demons.

I spent so much of my life in my vocation trying to say it right, and get it right; overestimating my influence and underestimating my power and impact. Surrounded by others, mostly women of great power, doing some version of the same. Yet, in my mind's eye, I look out at Lake Superior, the cold freshwater ocean that I knew in my childhood, where one can see the banks of Canada. I see the morning mist that covers the far shore, barely visible, as the dead sing to me ceaselessly, and I know very little of these worldly matters that once mattered so much. What matters to me is what we are building right now. We are constructing the vessels that carry not some elite few but all of us who are willing to keep living, into what comes next. This is not coming; it is already here. We are being reorganized, re-created, and remade: our only choices are in how we meet our destiny.

In our fear, we critique and cancel failing systems with failing leaders. I get it. We are not sure we have what it takes to be shipbuilders. We have no sea legs. We can't swim. We hate salt and sun and storms. We holler out to whoever will listen, that this is unfair; we want other options. We "Karen" the future. We want to speak to the manager. We want some-one in charge, even some tired greasy kid, to pay for how difficult and limited our choices are. The sea does not care. The fire does not care. The Mother of All does not care. The Baba Yaga grins at us, rattling her skulls, ignoring all com-plaints or attempts at dialogue. She says only one word: *choose*.

•••

It has been one of the hardest lessons of my life: to step back when I can do no better. The cultural realms around us, while deeply divided, don't reward their different camps with strong solidarity or community. Individualism and pri-vatization have eaten out the heart of spaces where we can remember together how to grieve. But we simply can't do it alone, we are far too weak, too lost.

•••

Monsoons have been flooding Phoenix, and my body wel-comes them: their cloudy, cool wonder in the summer of a climate cooked by crisis and change; the simple relief to my skin of windows open in the car. The only time in my life where the arc of days are like they were when my child was an infant. The routine of the hours with an infant; every-one who has done it knows it. You are counting the hours between feedings and sleepings, holding on for dear life because it is so precious, and so hard—a dream state. This is different but with the insularity and smallness of the windows of time, the necessity of routine has increased. My life is so small and murky—the smallest it has ever been. What I do each day, trying to find some purpose or differentiation in it from the day before when I can't think, barely talk, and do not feel much. I still visit with my closest friends. We go on small day trips; I stare at a little bit of different scenery.

Then it is morning. I wake up and it is somehow the day of my last chemotherapy treatment. In the beginning, I curated these experiences, heavy with a strange wonder that this was happening to me, a sense of the unknown. I have always liked the unknown, even a terrible unknown. It is the knowledge that makes chemotherapy so particularly terrible—you know what is coming.

At this point, I don't care anymore who goes with me. I don't care about any fanfare, in bed, half wishing I was just watching TV and not bothering to write. I'm probably going to die anyway, I reason; that idea used to make me want to write, but now it just makes me want to leave all the ignorance and unknowing of those around me behind. Even with my shitty attitude, loved ones circle around me with texts and small presents.

But this is the final trip (for now) to the underworld. The final chemotherapy treatment of any set of treatments is the worst. The worst pain doesn't stop today for me, it starts. It will be ten more days until relief starts to come until it dawns on me that I don't have to go back there, to that ward, to that tower of pain in the desert that reaches to the sky, solitary and so massive it has its own exit off the highway.

Yesterday, at the infusion center, when I went to the bathroom there was a woman my age in a wheelchair, holding her own bag of piss (or vomit, it was hard to tell). She sat behind me, as I washed my hands at the sink, and she looked at me in the mirror, caught my eye—no smile, no bothering with pleasantries, no shyness at what she held in her hands. Only that long look, the look from beyond, the look past all of this. My guess was she was on her way to meet her ancestors soon. This much time surrounded by dead people, I know she was dying. I don't know the experience of where she is, but I see where she is headed. It becomes easy to feel who is going soon and who is not.

I feel that similar energy, the slow giving it all up, piece by piece, around me often enough. I feel it on the street too. I feel it in the grocery store, where no one meets anyone's eyes. My house is packed with the spirits of dead people, they don't feel that way, rather than giving up, they feel like they are peering in or standing guard.

• • •

I remember a night, many years ago now, when my dearest friend loved me enough to say to me, "I see a fearlessness, a willingness to fly that comes to you in the work, and then such fearfulness in your personal life. I fear the distance between these two parts of you will tear you apart." It was one of the truest things anyone has ever said to me. It touched, and knew, a place inside of me that I did not know anyone could. It was a warm night in Alabama, outside a motel, and I was awed that she would say this to someone so stubborn, so set in her own story, so completely hell-bent on not seeing the truths in front of her. I remember, even through my bullshit, knowing that only true love would push her to say that. I heard her. I let her in. I went home and made moves.

I changed my life. I left a relationship. I lived alone again, above my grandmother's house, who was then still alive. I was raw and I was reckless, but I was not split in two. I opened the window in those upper rooms every night and put plants by the window. The place smelled of humid flowers, and occasionally of human shit, when I needed to go downstairs and wipe my grandmother when she had an accident in the middle of the night. The windows sat tucked between and beneath the Carolina Pines. I drank a lot and I had friends who I saw almost every day.

We went to bars and strip clubs often, and I would drive home, coming up the rickety backstairs, hoping those wooden planks would hold me just one more night. When I took off my bra there were parts of my paycheck, in one-dollar bills. I needed to live alone then and, thank God, I could do so. I stared at the wall a lot. I felt like my cells were regenerating. Eventually, I got stuck in my patterns again, as I tend to do. But I remember that time when I was holding the reins of my life looser and my hands were much less cramped.

•••

I remember a different afternoon, in a winter café, many years before living in those upper rooms in North Carolina. The late 1990s. I am fifteen years old and another dear friend looks at me across a table and says: "You have already slept with several girls, and I think maybe it might be a good idea for you to consider that you could be. . . bisexual." I tell her absolutely not. I am just experimenting. I leave the US for Eastern Europe shortly after, convinced of the story I tell myself rather than the truth in front of me.

Having been out now, for so many years, this story reminds me how I have had the ability since adolescence to look truths, even the most obvious ones, right in the eye and deny them. This has been a lifelong habit. It has cost me a great deal of time and pain. So, now I look to be set free of it. Truth—and truths—might be one of the hardest concepts to reckon with as I heal. For now, I just acquaint myself with the idea of trying to see what life is telling me plainly, instead of editing it with my own story.

We live actively surrounded, enveloped by denial. Denial all the way to death. The year is 2021, and it is killing us. But being judgmental of that denial is not saving individuals or the collective. I know, as well as anyone, the lies we tell ourselves are stories and stories are powerful. They work on us in places that are otherwise hard to reach, like the places where my cancer has lived, deep, dark, hidden—the sea caves of the body, so hard to reach from the shore.

Radical truth and transparency become the boat, the vessel to carry us out. I read somewhere that when drug counselors help addicts get clean, they recommend radical honesty about all things—like explaining why you are *really* five minutes late to a meeting. They say it can produce a euphoric effect. I try it. Then I walk around doing it all the time. Here's an example: I have written at least half this journal high. And when I say "high," I don't mean a joint or two. I mean opiates that have brought me to my knees with shame, dizziness, confusion, numbness, and depression. I mean being high in a way that one can barely walk, read, or write. I mean it is currently 1:15 a.m. and I only fell asleep at eleven, and I am writing this mostly to try to make it to my next fix at 2. The drugs, as much as the chemo, as much as cancer, have cut me off from everyone except those who immediately surround me. Even then, it is hard to reach them and for them to reach me.

The more one cycles in and out of these drugs, the more intense the withdrawals, and the more sinking the depression. This is the final round. I tell my dad, who will be seventy-three next month, "I would be happy to never touch an opiate again." We are walking each other around the block. It is a warm night with a big moon and both our legs are stiff. He says, "They have their place, Caitlin, they got you through." He is right. He has had reasons to use them, for a shorter time, himself. I approach nine months of a cycle of their use. They have filled me with lustless despair.

Yet, I wanted to write while on them. I want to write while using them still. This broken, using, waiting-for-the-fix part of me, is also me. But I know how many others, in my very own neighborhood, are broken and using them tonight. So why not tell the truth? Using like this, even only for this long, changed me. As I swim at the bottom of the ocean of my final treatment (I hope), I know I have been changed by other truths. When I thought I was going to die, I experienced the realities of cancer, drug use, and disability as my future; now they are part of my present, and that will shift too in the coming months. I am not sure how long I will have left after cancer treatment—once one has been in it, one realizes we can never know. All I know is the temporary nature of drug use and disability are now as powerful as addiction itself because I know that, on another path, they are not temporary for me.

During and after surgeries, I was fed intravenous fentanyl. It was very little and for a very short time and, yet, when I was high on it, I pictured my son and I did not love him. They told me I had ovarian cancer while I was on fentanyl. I said, stone-faced, "I told you so." I did not cry and I did not care. And I wondered later what others must feel every day to seek out fentanyl in order to feel nothing. To feel nothing—not *less* but a dusty, pale nothing. In her Earthsea series, Ursula K. Le Guin describes a place of death, a purgatory where you are stuck and unable to return to the earth, unable to become part of it again. A place where you look at your own children and do not know them or embrace them, a place of shuffling and quiet where the mountains are called Pain. When I picture fentanyl ticking quietly into my IV, I think of that place. I remember the night after surgery, silent in a bed on an empty hospital floor, knowing COVID patients lay dying in the wing below me. I dragged myself to the toilet to show the nurse I could use it alone so that he would let me go home, where I could feel something again, anything at all.

• • •

Up to this point in my life, there were so many ways to be alive in this body I had no idea about. I had no idea about crawling to the toilet because you can't walk. I had no idea about opiate withdrawal, where all you think is, "*Please don't open your mouth and tell everyone around you to shut the fuck up and stop clinking their forks.*"

No one around you wants to hear it, but when you are that deep into chemotherapy you feel only half alive. It is a terrible and strange place, but if I am honest, not a boring one. Like sitting astride a long border, leaning slightly towards the living side; or lying on the ocean floor, looking up at the light where it meets the water's surface. It's lonely, but even in the loneliness, I see how others who love me put on their own oxygen masks and fight their way down to the ocean floor, to my side. They grab my gilled and ugly mermaid hand, when I am breathing only water and poison, and share their air with me.

• • •

In my final chemotherapy session, still, at the very bottom of the bottom of my personal ocean, there is only one vein left they can find to use. It is on the top of my forearm, not even a big, juicy inner-arm vein. I sob as they drive the sheath and its needle through the skin of the third flower of my tattoo, one tiny ink line of the flower, the same shape and size as the vein beneath it, almost too small, giving the last of all it's got. It feels like being poisoned through a tiny tributary of my blood flow, not a river. It feels like that because that is what it is. I feel it burning up and through that arm. I look around at the six separate plastic bags hanging from my IV. I watch as the nurse takes off the hazmat gloves and smock. The large orange "biohazard" stickers on the fat plastic bags still reminding me of a zombie movie like the first time I saw them. But inside those bags is only what the yew tree made.

After the drugs go in, I notice my final chemo pod at least faces a window. The mountains high above the desert and highway are the color of ash and sand, silent and tall and hot and so foreign to me. I concentrate on them and on the eyes and face of the friend who has accompanied me. As I lose consciousness, I imagine eyes that have no eyelashes, as mine lack them now, eyes that see things so painfully and beautifully: nothing stays out, not dust, not light. I remember the week before when my child asked me why I wear sunglasses all the time now, and I told him, "Because I see everything, my sweet love. My eyes keep nothing out now. So I have to protect my eyes." He surprises me as I meet his eyes through sunglasses in the rearview mirror, because he does not ask his usual "Why?" but instead nods knowingly, the hint of a smile on his lips.

In my last chemo underworld sequence, floating in the big gray chemo chair, I dream of tigers in jungles I have never seen, stalking prey in trees so green they glow almost purple at their edges. In my dreams, they, like me, have nothing to offer this dying/changing/rebirthing world but their absolute rawness and realness, the power that I have come to see only true vulnerability brings. Living with your robe dropped perpetually around your feet. For beings like us, the only way forward is a nakedness tattooed with scars: the scars are the design, the scars are by design. Honor lies in those shapes. For the rest of my life, I expect I will struggle with this, hating to know my limits with such neon luminescence.

I have given so much to this process of poisoning. It could all be for five more years of life; it could be for twenty. In twenty years, if I live, I will be fifty-nine. I was willing to do it for fifty-nine, and I was willing to do it for forty-five. But I can't deny the truth that part of me knows having six to twelve months to live felt. . . clearer, neater, surer. Now, a messier, sober life awaits me, with many contradictions and few certainties. An uphill battle that will require strong lungs, strong heart, and pacing.

The same awaits all of us. We choose either to surrender and submit to it fully or swim against the stream.

Another night, up again. My aunt reminded me last week of the words of Thich Nhat Hanh, "Our actions are our only true belongings." How fucking beautiful. How terrible, if that is the case, so many of my belongings have been, how beautiful others. I picture them as physical objects, sitting with me in my house—perhaps because it is not yet 2 a.m., not yet time for more drugs, and my whole right leg wails a song of Fourth-of-July-sparkler pain. I need to think of something else for fifteen minutes.

Some of my actions/belongings ooze blood in their ugliness, others shine like abalone shells. Many of the most beautiful ones are fragrant plants braided together—the actions taken with others. There are some stored in the corner of the hot laundry room, their faces turned away from me because I still do not want to face them. But I know they are there. They see me and I see them; no hiding and no dark can cut our cord. If our only true belongings are our actions, then there will be more all the time. We will take them with us, right up to the last choices we make.

The repetition in this book makes me feel self-conscious and awkward, but it feels important, and it feels real. It mimics the forgetfulness, the fog, of my state of being itself. So, I will say again: I am not healed of this sickness. I pray for the strength to be reborn. I think how many women—how many humans, how many givers to the world—suffer this and are told "Get better. Feel better." It rings so false, in our hearts and in our minds. There is no old self to heal, there is no getting better. There is only rebirth or death. Some things, some people, and some parts of oneself can't get better, because things that "get better" are essentially the same.

I mimic the story I see for our world: at the dawn of the age we are now in, we need rebirth not reform. Overexposure will not heal our shame, sharing ourselves online with a world that we are already sure does not want us. It is the cessation of hiding; it is the coming clean that connects us.

•••

I read the newspaper in bed. It contains information too dense to hold about how some of us just want to die en masse, whether we know it or not. Some of us want the freedom to die, uncaring about how it affects others. Some of us don't believe in the outside world anymore, don't believe in what is around us. We want to take our chances with plagues. Critical and analytical minds, trained in academia, can't help us absorb these facts.

Yet, our essence, the essential space is in our bodies. Bodies know why. The flesh and blood of us know what is coming, just as the earth knows. At that basic level, we know what we live in now. Finding and connecting to what bodies know can be harder. So many of our bodies have been ignored for long, painful, hot centuries. Shunned, beaten, ignored, unloved, bitter, and yet renewing, bodies, moving through time and generations. We must find what is alive, what is waking, even if we will not be here for its full emergence. We are remembering that we are not the only living beings. We are not so consumed by the false promises of the private and privatized that we have lost the smell of what is alive, the taste for it.

Chaos is close: let it be—let us push our hands into it and turn each tiny locality more towards connection and raw realness. We won't be alone. No matter what comes.

The ways we were writing about and knowing the world, even ten years ago, feel profoundly naïve and antiquated now. I walk laps, when I can, in my air-conditioned gym, while the land is scorching outside. It all feels dead: the people, the faces, the machines, the building itself. I stumble up to the roof and the clouds are moving over dry, dry mountains. The rare rains of Phoenix. It's so alive, the tinny and corny music on the speakers is nothing, nothing, nothing compared to what awaits us.

Vandana Shiva speaks about awakening to the living earth and what it means to know that, with a hundred million microbes in our gut, our bodies are 90 percent not our own. It is not in any way metaphoric that we are part of the earth, part of each other. Travelers that feed me, travelers that I breathe, travelers keeping me alive. Not only poison travels through me and the medicine is not solely mine.

CHAPTER 8

Earth Under Every Floor, Autumn 2021

"Barn's burnt down—now I can see the moon."

Mizuta Masahide wrote this in the seventeenth century, and it is my favorite haiku ever. My youngest cousin, who I adore, thinks it is hilarious that this is my favorite haiku. She lies in bed with me, holding my sick hand, laughing because it is so weird to her. She's twenty-one and can remind me of what is truly funny and weird when I have forgotten. Before she goes back up north, she tapes a heart-shaped piece of paper with the haiku written on it to my bathroom mirror. I smile, thinking of her, every time I see it—which means every time I must wrestle with my appearance in the mirror. I meditate on it whenever I take a poisoned chemo piss, which must be one of the least respectable (not to mention least sanitary) ways to meditate. Every time I read it, I know it, I welcome it, and I let all past assumptions and stories go. If only for that brief painful moment, I see that moon in the place where the barn once obscured it in my life: big, naked, round, and never seen before. I feel grateful—me, who is so very tired of being told to feel grateful.

I stubbornly decide that only I get to decide when I feel grateful. Grateful is part of a triangle of acceptable cancer feelings that I resent having forced on me: gratitude, sadness, and peace. When they do come, I like them to come as suddenly welling springs, not because they have been prompted by myself or others. So, this gratitude doesn't feel like the sort you'd dutifully add to a gratitude list. It feels like satisfaction. Fine, the damn barn has burnt down: all my structure, all my story, all my plans. And, in the end, it was all in the way. I could not see, I could not hear, I could not move. With so much in the way, I could not even see that which I love the most, those whom I love the most. I could not let anything all the way in, because the barn needed to be stocked and lit, and there was never a sky without it consuming my horizon. But now, it lies in smoking ash, and I can see the moon, so insistent, so everything not of my making, construction, or design. When I can see the moon, I can also see everything around it.

There is nowhere to go but in and on.

• • •

This is a new time. If we find our raw truth, we are not simply replicating the past. We are no poor copy of everything that has been under millions of wide, bright days of sun. We have the chance to find our desire. I burn in my house and read article after article about how not only do we have fewer friends, less sex, and feel lonelier in this country, we even *want* less. We have lost desire, in every way one can measure such things. I hear the music of my ancestral homeland in winter—what we called our choirs or folk music: it is more our angels shrieking in passion.

I think about Prague and Berlin and Frankfurt Am Main covered in snow, the winter markets lit up, shining Christmas lights over those bridges, built hundreds of years ago. The Karluv Most, the Charles Bridge, which crosses the Vltava River in Prague was built in 1357, to replace the Judith Bridge, lost in a flood. The mortar that holds the bricks together in Karluv Most is made from eggs. I think of the hands that shaped the egg mortar and laid those bricks. I remember Christmas as a girl, then almost a woman, on that bridge. I was never dressed properly for the cold when I lived there, and I had an ancient gray-green leather jacket with leather buttons that I wore over my sweaters and sweatshirts all the time. I am still that girl, and I am not her.

Years spent in the US since then wallpaper over that memory—so precious, filled with longing for that land. Oh, to go back in time and stay there, to have chosen a different path, a harder one maybe, and perhaps sweeter. The US takes up all the oxygen, always thinking it is the only place that exists. Perhaps it is because it is a country so huge, settled, and colonized so thoroughly. I guard my memory, fiercely, privately all these years later, sure that only my mother would understand it and perhaps understand me better than myself. She was once a little girl crossing a huge ocean, leaving the entire universe of all she had ever known behind. Her lands are my lands—and they are not mine at all, I am the daughter born here in the US, dreaming always, always of the homeland—romanticized, forgotten, remembered, and always beyond reach.

I feel the lust for any empty courtyard of those dear, snow-covered lands. I desire it with every brow-beaten, metallic organ left in my body, and I laugh that it has taken this, this cancer, for me to finally stop trying to fit and belong. Now, I simply desire to live out the one clear path given to me. The Baba Yaga, the bone crusher, though I don't desire her presence, also lives where desire lives. She knows the price, and the consequences of desire, which makes desire even stronger. Desiring life itself is the desire that burns the hottest, messiest, tipping over everything, on its way to the door.

• • •

Every day in the year 2021, I am in some form of terrible pain. The pain is so far beyond anything I have known and so continuous that I know only some of you reading this can understand. Doctors say that chemotherapy is a form of torture, though they smugly remind you how much they have tempered the treatment over the years. An elder in Phoenix once told me that when he had chemo here in the 1970s, he would wake every hour in the night, get in his car, drive west ten miles through all the stoplights, then back east through them again, get out of his car, go in his house, take an ice cold bath, sleep twenty minutes, then get up and do it again. All night. He said he had to stop himself from screaming at and hitting his wife and kids. It can make you go there, I say, I can see how chemo could make you go there.

But, on the morning of August 27, 2021, I wake free of pain for the first time I can remember.

The night before, when the pain broke for the last time, I dreamed that my son and I were actually siblings, not mother and son, that we had been orphaned at the winter solstice (when I first got sick), and that in the place of our parents, in our house with us, stood the largest evergreen I have ever seen. She was giant and silent and ancient, with boughs of the darkest green. She had a deep darkness around her and, when I looked up at her, she shadowed the room. Although she was inside our dream home, she was alive, rooted through the floor into the earth itself. I knew that we must keep her alive, that she would parent us, keep us safe.

Though he and I live in the desert, she is the tree of my ancestors, she grows everywhere they grew and lived, on two different continents. Trees like that are always connected to the sacred time of silence in the white, white cold.

Anywhere we live, our ancestor trees can come to us. I know, stranger, whoever you are, that you might feel this can never be true again for you—that the laminate or tile or wood or cement under your feet could never be broken and grow such a mighty tree, that only opioid dreams bring such things. But a temporary heavy drug user like me knows a sober dream when it comes to me.

It was my sacred, and first, sober dream in a new life.

The sober dream's instructions feel clear: rebuild my life in this sea storm of time with that tree at the center. Water her, care for her, let her raise me up, don't take her for granted or let her suffer or die. *There is always earth under every floor*, she whispers to me.

The roots of the tree are always there.

The strength it takes to live again is the greatest cliché of any illness that brings you near death. It is true, to a certain extent, but it is not only the strength of the body. (I hear my father tell a friend, also in his seventies, "Watching Caitlin, I don't think you and I could do it, at our age.") Knowing what would make one give up living, seeing the edge of the far-off abyss, peeking over, is also the surrender that shows me the incredible earthly delights I am willing to live for.

The pandemic/plague around the globe, and my own personal plague, have cocooned me so thickly, that I would be lying to say I do not fear coming back into the world. Yet, I lust for it. The desire I feverishly pray for is for the awakening of the world, for the world to be freed from its bloodthirsty numbness—which is what I finally wish for myself. I think about all I will do with the use of my legs, hands, and arms (marked forever by the tattoos that mark this time). I think about the joy I will feel at growing hair again. Let alone eyebrows.

I think far less about what I will do with my mind, it feels eclipsed—a black sun in June—by the unfurling leaves of my plans for my now wide-open, messy, and spontaneous heart.

I promised my son that, when the weather changed and got cooler, my hair would grow. A bet made at a time when

I could not imagine winning it. Yet, it does. The magic of growing new eyelashes and eyebrows is quick and strange. My hairless body grows fine hair everywhere again, under the light of a full moon, like a werewolf. Suddenly my skin is rough everywhere, short hair standing up on my arms, even when I am calm. I am shining and crave fun. I want to be the fun ambassador again as I called myself in my twenties when I lived in North Carolina. I dye the fuzz on my head platinum blond and eat constantly: I say the names of the foods that I feel bring my body back to me: pecans and cranberries and kale and salmon and hamburger buns and tuna and tart green apples.

When asked about chemotherapy, I joke now that I would not recommend it to anyone who is not 100 percent sure they want to live. But, of course, I am not joking.

My partner and I put on wigs and ride bikes around on Halloween, like teenagers. Make out under streetlamps. I do yoga and sit outside watching trees change. I say aloud, with my neighbors staring at me: "Audre, I think I finally get erotics, and why to you, to someone who went through what you did, it would become everything—the life force, the thing that matters beyond death."

I don't worry, but I have fear. One night I can't find my son at the park for three and a half minutes, and the fear that stays with me for three days keeps me awake at night. But I don't worry. And I have stopped pretending to worry, as though it gives me some badge of vigilance.

I have memory loss. But that's not so bad. Some of it's gone, dates and times certainly, but also how hard and personally I used to take life sometimes. That is forgotten too, and that is just fine. The posturing, the holding back, the denying of what is true, the trying to force things that are not meant to come and stay together—all forgotten. I am sure some of it will creep back in, but I bask in the absence of old demons. These are losses I can handle.

I have enough memory. I remember my kid's face, my life's work, and those I am lucky enough to do it among, my most private visions, the view of the world from the old-world buildings of my ancestral homeland, all those I have loved, no matter the pain those memories bring. I'll take the memories I have and not worry too much if I can't remember what day it is—who gives a fuck about that anymore?

I struggle to edit the first part of this manuscript, because every time I do, I weep. It is close, so close to being ready for other's eyes, I feel it in my bones. It is October, I am dragging my feet, I can feel it. It came to me one night that the first portion must be done by Halloween. As the veil between shape and form, living and dead, begins to thin, I realize that no matter what happens now, this part is done for me. I still can't feel my left foot; I still must wait to see if the cancer is in my lymph nodes, if it will come back if I need radiation. But my fate is changed because how I meet it, abide it, how I take life itself, is changed.

As Ursula K. Le Guin wrote at the end of her Earthsea trilogy, "There is no safety. There is no end. The word must be heard in silence. There must be darkness to see the stars. The dance is always danced above the hollow place, above the terrible abyss."

One day, I am driving in the car, with the top down, the sun slicing a searing line on the horizon as it prepares to set. "*Oh, Caitlin,*" I think to myself, "*you don't have to be all deep about it now. You just have to be wide.*"

The weather finally agrees with me, cool and bright, and I think about how the dead crowd around when one is close to their threshold. When one comes firmly back to life, they recede. As they return to waiting their voices are quieter, and more effort is required to hear them. I begin to get better, at least my body does. My eyebrows are thick, like a raccoon's. They feel luxurious on my face. My eyelashes grow back, but perhaps will never be as long. Hot flashes still plague me, day and night, but medications help. Unfortunately, no longer using opioids can make life both boring and raw sometimes. Now that I am fully transitioned off them, it is better, but I still have moments of returning to my same demons and routines where I think: *Is this all there is? Is this all I come back to?*

Old grudges return, they do not evaporate. They must be worked through and then worked through again. Progress is made tiny step by tiny step.

I decide not to do radiation. I still have one enlarged lymph node. The doctors talk the options through with me for hours. I touch on the familiar feeling of talking to them, keenly aware of how their training in methods for talking to cancer patients makes the conversation so circular, gentle, and restrained. At the end of the day, I decide not to have radiation because it could affect my bowels, and having bowel problems is very high on my list of visceral and practical fears. I also just don't want to feel that damn tired. So, I say no, I tell them that I don't want to come to this tower, this part of the city for a few months. They accept this.

I go to corny yoga classes at my gym, which help me profoundly. Three times a week to feel my left foot again. I have spent months looking down at my left foot from the corner of my eye, to make sure it was walking in line with my right: more than once I looked down and it was bleeding because I could not feel it being cut or stubbed. I learn that the feeling in muscles and joints does not come back all at once. I stretch the foot literally hundreds of times: walking, in the morning in bed, at night in bed. Slowly, I feel it again. I feel where it touches the ground. I feel the heel and the arch and the bones inside of it.

I am my "old self" again and not again. I talk often and loudly. I debate. Get excited. I say things I regret on impulse again. But I am also changed. I move through emotions more quickly and have more boundaries. Steady myself. I care a great deal less about a lot of things. I return to work slowly, but its impact does not make me as heavy. I am less dutiful. I seek my best contribution and offer it—the rest I leave to others. The country is numb and chaotic; the energy is of a person bracing themself, head down. The news is full of murder in all its forms; the country feels suicidal and homicidal on every level. Natural death seems on the decline: so many men wanting to take themselves out of this world and bring so many people with them.

I am back to being stuck in certain resentments, walking out arguments and grievances in my head when I wake up with hot flashes in the middle of the night. I feel disappointed—as I have gotten better, as life has become again both loud and mundane, I had hoped to continue to be removed from the habits of my mind that I struggle with most. But I am sober now, not using opioids, so clearly, nothing feels as placid. I had hoped the habits would be shed—with my new bone marrow, new shape, and if not new skin, at least new hair on it. These changes were nothing short of miraculous: my arms absorbing lotion again, my eyelashes shielding my eyes from wind and sun again. So, I suppose I had subconsciously hoped for the same new growth when it came to my mind. But pettiness and irritations returned. Here comes some of the baggage again, rearranged. Some are missing and evaporated, but some of it is still there.

But I do see things differently when I sit still. When I am quiet, I feel my new shape: so round and full. And, when I tighten back into an arrow, I can release myself from that shape more quickly. The progress is tedious and repetitive, but I open out into a bowl more and more often.

I stabilize my peace. I say what I think. I slowly begin to make plans for life again. Interestingly, I start to think about what I really want for the next twenty years, and what

I want to put into place now. I go on planes every now and again, but it exhausts me, and my feet and knees lock up for days. It is hard to be well enough to go back to work, but not as well as I was before. I cannot remember or concentrate without prep time and decompression time, and this is hard to explain to most of the people in my life, who see me as simply back to being me again. I buy a townhouse, the sheer buying of it a Hail Mary. It happens only when I have given up that it will. On the day that I know for sure it will be ours, we drive by it and my son says from his car seat, "Thank you, Mommy, for buying us a house." I can remember few moments in my life when I have ever felt so powerful, so certain, so proud. I am the man of my dreams.

I move my son and me into the new place and fill it with plants. I leave the hot, cozy, bright cottage of my cancer behind, with its deep, narrow bathtub that holds much comfort and much pain. Later, I will learn that, within a year, the cottage itself begins to actively fall apart—plumbing backing up, termites in the walls, the pipes around the house having to be ripped out of the ground. It crumbles and quickly becomes uninhabitable. I imagine it as Baba Yaga's cottage in the forest, falling into the earth when she steps away.

I will always remember the bathtub of that cottage. It was the place I soothed my son through each transition, even before cancer, and I will always remember it that way. But it was also the huge enamel bowl where I sat on my knees sobbing after all my hair fell out and it needed to be shaved, asking that no one speak or look at me for a long time.

I struggle with this manuscript; it feels like the story of something that happened to another person. It is hard to integrate and square up the then and the now. For months, I could not be talked into reading what I have written so far, let alone editing it. I am like a mule being pulled down a mountain trail. I am just not ready.

CHAPTER 9

I Want To Know What Love Is, Spring 2022

As I write about this season, I am over the Atlantic Ocean. *My joy, my joy, my secret spring of Joy,* I say to myself. I head towards my mother/land. She is already there, my mother, waiting for me with her cousins and family and my father, drinking a bottle of wine. My little cousin, who is not so little anymore, will be married. I love her so much that one late night in a rainy bar in Berlin I took off the earrings she admired and gave them to her, kissing her knuckles before saying goodbye. Her mother did the same once for my mother when she was heading back across the ocean. I remember as a little girl watching her mother take a round, gold heart off her own throat and put it on my mother's. Her mother died during the pandemic, so the wedding will not be what it might have been, but I have moved logistical, financial, and parental heaven and earth to be here.

My cousin's father is my favorite. He is the uncle I remember pushing me up hills on my bike as a girl. To live to see him again means so much to me that I weep when I should be sleeping on the plane, weep until my mask is wet and the flight attendant looks at me strangely. Yet, to live to see him again when he has just lost his wife also somehow feels like all of this has felt: being spared with a cost, the Baba Yaga standing in the moonlight of the open door.

My flight is taking me to my mother and uncle's hometown, right in the center of Europe. A city that tourists don't care for: it is big enough, but not a beauty, per se. Our family graves are there, and the street whose name means "Free People Street," where the mother of my own mother's heart lived—my Tante Luise, and where I spent pure and true moments of my childhood. The city is crisscrossed with the same timeworn trains I wanted my ashes scattered from if I did not survive cancer. Instead, I will ride them again in this little body that has lost and given me so much and is still here in this form.

The world is changing, deeply and profoundly. I already have changed and I cannot change back. I can forget for moments and go back to old habits and traces of bitterness, but each week, like clockwork, some moment passes, and it resets me.

My cousins asked me over email what I wanted to do with the ten days I had squeezed out of my wildly busy life, this unlikely gift of days I had given to myself, free of all responsibilities except those to my mother's kin. "It will sound stupid," I said, "but just kiss and kiss and kiss the ground of my precious spirit home, where I lived and loved as a girl and thought I would never see again."

The vampires of Eastern European lore must sleep deep in the soil of their homelands to be well again. I have always imagined that I felt a similar longing, a similar need to reset, to touch those walls on the street as I walk by them, to sit on the ground by the rivers. The buildings are so old, a few of them the ones wherein my ancestors dwelled. I feel comforted to think of Alice Walker and her idea that we are never the first to live, suffer, or die and how my ancestors lived, sorrowed, suffered, loved, and died within the walls of these large, gray apartment buildings I touch now. Of course, this land is changed too, yet again— newly slick and thick and covered in blood, just miles away from the billowing dust of the war Russia has been waging in Ukraine.

I think of the melting glaciers in Alaska and other places, and how we use gas-powered ships to see them with our own eyes, even as they disappear, even as the emissions from our ships speed their melting. We long to see them once as we kill them. And yet, I am one of those who still wants to see the glaciers.

We are not alone. But sometimes we are the only ones with our eyes open. The dead are not like the numb. They are active and moving and sometimes clamoring. That is how I have felt them. When I was near death, I yearned for my mother's lands, and I have no real idea why. Now that I will soon see them, be alive to see them, I yearn for them even more. How we love what we love has no rhyme or reason, it simply is. But perhaps there can only be brief moments of lucidity for a species as far gone as ours. So, we must plan accordingly—as the dying often do, preparing for the cycle to turn again. One day we can glimpse the whole picture and, the next day, go back to pretending.

• • •

I am here now. I am here. I wanted to live beyond cancer to be here again. It was one of the things on my non-hypothetical bucket list. In the United States, is my work. My loves. My vocation. My son. My callings. My contributions. Here, particularly in Eastern Europe, being and living has always been enough for me. I don't have to do anything. I am. I don't have to have an opinion. I don't have to get it up to give what I have again and again. I revel in simply being: walking, eating, talking, touching the ground. I put my phone away.

A person rarely at peace, I am at peace. The ground gives me energy and allows real rest. My cells want the food—the bread, the coffee. My aunt and uncle's home feels so easy. Their daughters don't live here anymore, so I have my own room, with a balcony on the glorious garden. Colossal spruce trees tower above the flowers and lawn. My uncle makes the "green sauce," the specialty of this region, the region of my mother's and my grandmother's accents, the sounds of Hessen in Central Germany. We laugh trying to remember the seven herbs that go in the sauce, a list that kids in this state are supposed to memorize.

I am in complete wonder at how my mother's mother tongue bubbles up in me—a gift of childhood language acquisition—and words flow back to me effortlessly. Without trying they come forth: imperfect, messy, bad grammar, and understandable.

We go back and forth between languages, and I understand both. A unique experience for me in a life filled with English and Spanish when I don't speak Spanish and typically only understand half of what is said around me. There is some mental and spiritual completeness to understanding the gist of all conversations. Both parts of me are made whole, my mother's and father's sides, as talk swings one way so my aunt feels comfortable and then the other direction so my father will also understand. It is a lazy linguistic pendulum that has been familiar to me since childhood.

We bike for hours in the village, then by playgrounds, fields, and creeks. It stays light until almost ten, and I think about how strong I have become since finishing my cancer treatment. How strong my legs and thigh muscles are pumping on the bike. I think of the time when I would not have been able to balance on a bike, when I could not speak even one language, let alone two—three if I include Czech, my favorite to make long, ridiculous, grammatically incorrect drunk speeches with. I remember the summer of quiet, burning hell when even my inner voice was not talking. At that time, I had no language—I who so loves talking. I have compartmentalized cancer to survive the process of coming back fully to life. But, here, on this land, I am strong and sure-footed enough to remember it. The process is like its own subtle form of coming back to life, taking root in my mother soil. I am a watered plant that raises itself up overnight while the household is sleeping.

•••

We have dinner beside fields and wildflowers and other patrons eating and smoking. My littlest US-born cousin is working on her bilingualism now that she has graduated college and is sniffing around for what else life has to offer. We debate the translation of the word *lieblingstadt*. I maintain in English that it is not a "favorite city." "That doesn't do it justice at all!" I say. "It is 'the city of my heart,' 'love-city,' 'city that is my sweetheart,' 'darling-city'—something like that!" We laugh. I am usually a bad translator, but they must concede that I am right—the word is lost in translation, and no English word comes even close. My mother says, with tears in her eyes: "This place is my *lieblingstadt*. It does my soul good to come here."

The city of her birth, the city of her mothers, the city where she was mothered, and the city from where she was taken across the ocean in a ship for some strange promise of new life.

I was on psilocybin one day—after my diagnosis but before chemotherapy. I had a six-hour visitation from women ancestors on my mom's side. They told their stories and I wept until wrung out. Their sorrow was so deep. I distinctly felt like they wanted their stories unburied, to speak aloud. They wanted their boils lanced and their grief released. There's a difference, I have found, between being a conduit for pain and bearing it for others. A conduit is like a metal rod for lightning: it passes through you and into the earth. Bearing unexpressed pain, though, is where we risk stagnating: the waters of grief stand until they fester and smell. There is a similar bottling-up of the pain involved in the immigration experience.

There is a renaissance of immigrant stories being written now. These stories often contradict the accepted and dominating norm: voices for immigrants who are not always so grateful to assimilate are not eager to disappear into some version of the "American dream"—pushing against a colonial river current to tell more nuanced and nonbinary stories of moving across oceans, lands, time. There is even a feeling of pushing against the dominant tide when one tells a different story about cancer, one where we are not serene and grateful, but often left with the bitterness of living with new boundaries and new strengths simultaneously. I thought recently how glorious it is that a new generation is awakening to how gender is nonbinary. We must also push further to understand that life itself and everything that makes up its contents are non-binary also, all things in the dawn and twilight grays.

I think of the adage, "When we know better, we do better," but life has never shown me this is true: we can know a great deal and stay stuck and unmoving. Rebirth brings new realms of knowledge, and I often resent the energy that comes up through me, driving me to be stronger than I ever was before I was sick. Sometimes, it is hard to move. Sometimes, I just don't want to.

In the past year, I have felt lonely at times in my strength: lonely in having to find my path, to find what I want for the rest of my life. No partner's life goals to hide behind (my old pattern), to submerge myself in. I am lonely as I hold the line on old patterns, relearning, again and again, to say *no* and *not again*. I love the townhouse I bought this spring, especially sharing one wall, a yard, and a garden with other people in the complex. It makes me feel less alone, a lifelong nomad committing to a place. I have filled the house with plants, though some like living with me better than others.

Today, I look out from my balcony as the German sun comes up at 5 a.m. and wonder about the names of the plants in my aunt's garden—something I would have had no interest in before cancer. I want to walk among the plants in this village outside the city many more times again as I age. I no longer need to be in the hustle and bustle to feel alive and at home. I would like to bring my son here to climb in the rugged wooden European playgrounds that Americans think are unsafe, and that are much more fun. I would like him to have his first beer here as a teenager; I can picture him drinking it—a smile on half his lips, sheepish and smug.

• • •

Since he could walk, my son has been obsessed with trains. He loves to build and take apart the blond wooden tracks in every room in the house. Recently, I convinced him to surround the trains at home with plastic trees and cows and chickens, and one plastic German Shepherd. He trumpets the song of a train whistle and I play the part of the dog howling at the train at night. I also love trains, the way they move, the way it feels to be carried in them. Unlike my cousins, for whom trains are a nonromantic necessity, I have no mundane train memories—only magical and cathartic ones. They think it is hilarious that I love them so much.

On the train to Berlin, I take meticulous pictures of the train for my son, and then I look at pictures of Hannah Arendt's eyes in a book. She is newly popular in the United States, enjoying a renaissance. Her work is like a giant, smooth stone that I turn over again on a path to reveal its face. How sad and still and dark her eyes have always looked to me. Yet, how they changed as she got older. In one black and white photograph from 1963, when she was fifty-seven, she is holding a cigarette, with an expression that seems to say "It is what it is"—her eyes so sad, her eyebrows almost vertical, like two black parentheses around her face.

Arendt warned that when people become "atomized"—lonely, feeling they belong nowhere and to no one—totalitarianism will often rise. Her eyes always ask me from the page or screen: Where is the line? When is it too much? How do we know when it will all turn upside down? How close are we to that line? What are the signs? Her words warn against arrogance. It can all change so fast.

Perhaps, these are the political lessons that cancer has given me. How flexible one must be to be strong, to "face it." How even then, strength can be a matter of crawling along. It can be humiliating, arriving only at the expense of pride. We must be able to change our approach and switch tools but stay the course. We must engage, because no matter how good holding ourselves apart and above feels in the moment, loneliness kills us.

"Atomized" is how I feel most days now. Some of it is cancer, the near-death experience, and some, I assume, is the spiritual and political climate of the US, the country that has given me my life, my loves, my purpose—but for which I have no love and never had any. At best, I've had affection for some regions. In this I share the sentiment of thousands of immigrants, and children of immigrants, who enjoy the indulgence of a lifestyle that is uniquely, luxuriously middle-class US America but who feel that, under the shirt and within the chest, there is no soul—at least not one that we can detect, our ancestors buried so far away. In my motherland, I feel like an outsider, at least when not with family—that babbling brook of mixed languages and cultures—but it is a relatively peaceful outsider status, surrounded by people who look like me—in whiteness and sometimes in uncanny ways around the eyes or the shape of the face. We tease how my mother and youngest cousin got the Polish face; the rest of us in the family who live in the United States have only a vague hint of it.

•••

In Western Poland, after many vodkas, lying in a bed and looking up at ancient, restored walnut rafters, I think about how my baby is in the West and my heart always pulls East. But my baby is fine, at Disneyland, not thinking of me. I watched a video repeatedly of him on a ride in a dark tunnel, his face still and filled with wonder, just moving his head back and forth like a hilarious little doll—a chatty and loud child stunned by wonder into a dazzled silence. I think how, the last time I was here in Poznań, Poland, I wasn't sure of almost anything in my life, my left hand hiding from, and not talking to, my right. That was before I was sick.

I wonder, matter of factly, if I am dead and not lying here in bed drunk and torn. I still want my ashes here, east of the former Iron Curtain, no matter when or where I die. I picture them, gray and unassuming, in the grass by the river Warta. I close my eyes and see them again, now in the river Vltava that runs through the center of Prague. I picture them flying from the train from Berlin to Prague. Any scenario would do. If they settle back into this earth, that earth should be here. I will never know why I love the bricks, the smells, the dumplings, the drunks, the way the windows open, and the hot, purple, thin-broth borscht, an elixir of bright life, cooked with the bones of a deer from the neighboring wood.

I picture the spell cast around me in the desert when I was sick—the spell of distant birch trees and evergreens and rivers. The last time I was in Poland, I had no reason to think about my death. It was not real to me. I had no proximity to it. So, it is not that surprising I had no idea what I was living for, or at least not exactly. I had been following my nose all my life and not knowing or needing to explain myself.

I am certain about my life—sometimes resigned, sometimes electrified, alternately trudging or gliding, but certain. Earlier today, we met Kenny from Baltimore in a gay bar as friendly as any I have ever seen: a real neighborhood place. Kenny has been in Poznań for six years after moving here for his boyfriend. I ask him how he feels living here. He says he misses his family and the food, but it is much better than being a Black gay man in the US. He shrugs. I comment on how much the US loves itself, and believes that, of course, everyone wants to stay there, no matter what, because that is where "it all happens." What happens there is a lot of killing, he points out. I agree. I say the word "cruel" is one I often hear about the US from people I meet and know who are not from there and do not live there.

This might be the first trip in my life where my mother's and father's sides of the family feel integrated, with neither romanticized. My family is just who they are, ordinary, at least in their context. And I am just a part of them—neither diminished nor rose-tinted. At one point, one of my uncles asks me why I want to go to a particular place. It is not very beautiful—that street, that apartment building—he says. I agree that it is not beautiful, but it is a part of me, so I want to see it. I am here and I exist.

I tell my cousin, at a different bar in Poznań, I never met a country or a culture that likes a Halfling: mixed culture, mixed race, mixed parentage, mixed languages. None of us are enough of any *one* thing for those who imagine they are somehow pure. Yet, the number of children mixing the divisions and labels of the world in their very own bodies, is increasing worldwide. In many different ways, with many different consequences for them in all their different contexts. I have read research that says when these children are asked which parent they feel their identity is most understood by—they say neither. Neither gets how it feels to be me, they say. There was a period of my life where I skulked around my fatherland and motherland feeling inadequate for either. Cancer taught me otherwise.

I am nothing. I am everything. I am not half of anything as it turns out. Not part this or that, just whole and boring.

I take a walk by the river Warta by myself. I thought wholeness would feel so fulfilling—a unifying lens. But there is only this river, the trash nearby. I kiss the ground. Polish construction workers stare at me strangely. Perhaps that is why this book is working when others I have tried to write haven't. She has come out whole. She is not naïve, and she tries hard not to be jaded. I am writing just for one other mother, one other queer, one other immigrant daughter, one other halfling, one other leader, and another broken person surviving cancer. I can picture a reader, and I am not afraid of what she thinks: she will take what works for her and leave the rest.

It gets cold by the river, so I get up and head on. Reveling in the shiver since the desert usually burns me so severely. Maybe this is all there is to it, this being *all in*, this being so whole and ordinary. It starts with adrenaline and fire and passion and surgery and drugs and suffering, and it ends here, not worried about time or measurements, not worried about horizons, *all in* for the train ride, the cobblestones, the child, the vodka, the new hair, the new growth.

●●●

Night falls in Poznań, and we revel in the public life of the town. My cousin says the US has no public life. Not true! I tell her we like to buy things together in the same air-conditioned spaces while not talking to each other or making eye contact. We double over in drunk hysterics. Everyone in the US is trying to look beautiful, I say, but no one is *looking*. No one is paying attention. We laugh so hard, remembering her years living with me in the US, in a little apartment in Atlanta. We recall the day she told me she was returning home because she just couldn't stand the cars one more year—among one million other things she no longer wanted to suffer. Most of it, though, had to do with the empty chests beneath the suit jackets, I think. Not a heartless place maybe, but one where it is hard to locate a heartbeat. At the time, I felt I understood her completely. Go home for me, for you, for us, I told her. Tonight, I tell her that, when I had cancer, seeing her again was on my bucket list. She looks up at me, grabbing my hand, her eyes so dark in the dark she almost looks angry. All she says is, and here we are, *schätzchen*, my sweetheart.

The summer evening wind picks up, and the bar across the street plays the 1980s American band, Foreigner. I hear the lyrics wafting down the street:

I can't stop now; I've traveled so far, to change this lonely life
I want to know what love is; I want you to show me

"We have shown you, now go live," comes the answer from somewhere underneath the uneven cobblestones, from all around me, from the rafters and the bells and the Slavic laughter of young people at dusk.

● ● ●

Inevitably, as is common on these visits, something begins to seep out of me as we head back west, to Berlin, from where I will head to Frankfurt Am Main and then to the US. On the westbound train, I let the land soothe me, trying to hold the red pines and the birches and the tall deep damp green grasses in my eyes from the train window. We pause for a long time at the Polish border. I catch my breath when the train moves again. I am ready. I have much to return to in the West, much to do with many people, and much in motion that I can bring different and better to.

•••

Berlin is Germany's capital of outness—in a country and world where so many remain closeted. This has made the city feel vital to me. I happily shiver in the cold summer morning—I think of the women I would see in the supermarket in hot Phoenix summer—their wigs sliding off their sweating bald heads. Everyone knows I wanted to whisper to them; everyone knows we are sick. I wanted to tell them they are not broken, not disgusting, not unlovable, just very sick. A sickness that is, at its core, about overproduction: so rest, reveal, I would want to say to them. Rest and show others what tired is, what spent is, what sick looks like. It doesn't make us ugly or wrong.

They looked so tired. So worn and slippery and ashamed. And yet, did I really accept that advice to see ourselves as enough? No matter how many times I gave it to myself? After personal rejections and years of fielding constant, heartless, spineless "feedback" as a grassroots progressive leader, and after years of keeping my head down "doing the work," did I believe it about myself? I did not.

It took deeply considering my death to see my own consequence as a person. I am not a person of "worth," a term that feels too close to capitalist value, calculating, and monetary. I am a person of consequence, and consequences come to me, not punishment.

In Berlin, I like to go alone to the canal near my cousin's apartment in the morning and stuff my face at one of the restaurants that are built on barges over the water itself. Since the morning is cold, only one Berliner is braving it. She is dressed in dark, conservative clothing and black leather boots. She is drinking a beer, a pack of cigarettes on the table before her, and a fluffy, lion-colored ten-pound dog at her feet. The dog is lying on the deck, listening to the water. As I boarded, I noticed a small, white ferry, its paint old and worn. She has a name in iron-colored paint on her side: the same name I would give a daughter if I had one. I look at the children feeding swans on the shore, wandering in the grass in those drunken circles that serve as the gait of two-year-olds everywhere. I let myself realize I want this imagined daughter, the pull for her has never gone away through cancer. I want to have her ravenously; I have the urge to hold her in my arms. I want to parent her alone if that is how fate decides it, no matter what anyone thinks.

I see her here. I see how I might be with her, different than I am with my son. How I might lean into the sleepless nights, the unpredictability of them, knowing from experience that I would survive them. I realize these are the aspirations of a fully living person and that I am shaking off the final vestiges of someone with one foot in and one foot out of life. I shed more of my half-deadness into the canal, leaving it in the water near the ferry.

On the shore, dipping willows grow five feet from the water, trimmed so neatly. How German. Weeping queers with long hair cut short of union with the water. Queer trees crying forever, while the rest of the city has the sly and resilient joy of our people everywhere. Perhaps the willow's job in this ancient city is to remember. You celebrate, you stay alive, we will remember and weep, they say.

Queerness, so present and complicated in my bloodline, has been a lifeline—a source of wild new life—a worth-the-risk way of living for me. I did not spend much time when sick, considering that most of the people who kept me in it and alive were queers and my blood family. The best aspects of being gay—the sly humor, the dirty joke, the intimacy beyond straight-laced intimacy—carried me back into life.

•••

This is also the first trip here when I have not secretly, nostalgically, or romantically wished to be more of something—my mother, my father, more from here, more from the US (so I would be happier there). I suppose I have outgrown being melodramatic and a bit tortured and spoiled: but I will shamelessly admit that took decades. Or perhaps it took cancer.

I order a sweet Danish to take with me for my cousin because delighting her is delightful. My American accent is strong enough that the server (a hearty woman working in a café that sways with the water) asks me if I am sure I want it and sure that I want it to go. I am certain, I tell her. So certain. *Nie so sicher in meinem leben.* Never so certain in my life, I whisper to myself.

Yes, it is true, I have never known a country or culture kind to halflings, but I am a Phoenix not from Phoenix who resides in Phoenix. I don't care much if those around me understand me; I don't need to be understood by strangers.

The gift of this trip is new to me: this ordinary wholeness. I marvel not at miraculous, immigrant things but at the things I remember—words, phrases, streets, foods. I don't care that I speak like a child, like a teenager, but I do remember being both here. The young girl they affectionally called *Imperialistka* (the little imperialist girl) in Prague, the name given for my US father and birthplace in the US.

I marvel at how things heal. What an overused and misunderstood verb: *to heal*. It doesn't mean simply "to fix"—us, our relationships, the world around us. Some things, especially these days, cannot be fixed.

I have always had limited patience for healing. Like most of us, I came into my cancer diagnosis just wanting to be fixed. Yet, instead of fixed organs, I have missing ones. Instead of fixed blood, there is new blood that has endured poison. Instead of fixed veins, I have veins that will never be the same. Instead of fixed bones, I now have new bone marrow. Never one to get the hint, I suppose it took a body with this many new and changed parts to heal.

CHAPTER 10

Long-Haul Healing, Spring 2022

I head back to the United States, alone, making the long journey West and North over the coldest part of the Atlantic Ocean. The peace I felt during my visit was sustenance, my body filled with a quiet joy warmed over an outdoor stove. Cancer has taught me to do my best to leave what is mine to leave on the dance floor. There were specific grievances and memories that I had to deliver home, the sentiment I was still a vessel for. I left what I needed to leave in the arms of my family, one by one. I left it by the rivers; I left it on the trains. I left it in the pines and gardens where I was a child. One of my aunts teased me that she could put up the old wooden swing again to match a photo of me as a young girl thirty-five years ago. I left what I needed to leave in the wooded and vine-covered cemeteries where my ancestors are buried, some of whom I knew and loved.

During the ten-day trip, I told the truth or others told it. Every tiny detail, no fibs, and no white lies. Long conversations, no phones. There is something about that kind of time that brings you back to life, to self, to others. I told the truth and I left the rest of the pain and the poison and the grief little by little so as not to overwhelm any one place, relative, or ancestor.

I left what was left of the sickness when I saw it in their eyes. I left it when I let their compassion in, compassion that doesn't overstate feelings, doesn't exaggerate, doesn't say "I love you" all the time. When I saw how they looked at me, so moved that I was still here, far more updated on my health situation than I had known—so European, quietly informed, and understated. They simply held me tighter to them.

• • •

Back in the States, I continue the strange and slow work of healing. Only 35 percent of women with ovarian cancer live more than ten years after their diagnosis. I have lived not much more than a year since my diagnosis. I could have nine years to go. I could have forty. No one knows—but at least I know I don't know. Things look good right now. I can run until sweat pours down my face, and I can drink three cocktails if I like without getting dizzy. I can carry my son's almost fifty-pound, sleep-warm body up and down the stairs.

My love for him remains as bright and dazzling as it was when I was sick, and I return to a normal state of mind for parents of young children, nauseous at the idea of losing him or him being hurt in any way.

In addition to a tiny amount of radical literature from the perspective of those with cancer, there is even less about the healing from cancer, the coming back to life that some of us do. We must climb a wall to rejoin the living. In a way, we do it in as much solitude as cancer treatment itself. It is hard to describe precisely how the days become refashioned together, one following another. It is hard to explain how one begins to *believe* again, somehow quickly and slowly, in a chronology, a future.

Strangely, I have long-term plans for my life in a way I never did in my old life. The division of my living years feels tangible and stark: there was before cancer diagnosis and after cancer treatment. There was one life and now there is another, though they may look alike.

I re-enter the times that we live in, a spooked, guarded chaos politically and spiritually. Doors close at night and people are burning inside. Denial has crossed into profound divergences of reality; people have crafted different stories to deal with our time. I think about my political commitment to write down the raw details of cancer often left out, a nod to feminist elders and political giants who showed us how the personal is political. I believe they never wanted that phrase to be overused or used selfishly. Pain is personal and political. It is not individual, not ours alone, but deeply, deeply personal. Political is simply the part that seeks to know and work with others, live among others, and not pretend we each exist on our many private islands.

I reread this book, this book I have written, and I keep writing her, in shock that someone wants to publish her. I am happy she exists. I try to remember that she is my book, not written by someone else. She is messy, personal, and chronological. Don't worry, they tell me. She is closer to being ready to be published than you think. She is readier than I am, I think, to be out in the world.

I think about cancer now that I, ironically, feel well enough to think differently about it. It is an ancient disease, called "the emperor of all maladies," by Siddhartha Mukherjee in his book of that name. But it is also an incredibly timely one. I don't just mean that one in three women will suffer it in their lifetime.

It is a disease of overproduction. Overproduce is what it does. How do we heal from a disease that does that in a society obsessed with excess and overproduction? Cancer is an inability in the body to decipher between healthy and unhealthy cells. It is a disease without boundaries, a system that uncontrollably spawns its deadly and damaging products.

I consider the multiplying, unrewarded love and sorrow of my maternal ancestors, their pain a map that spreads across the ocean. For what, I wonder blasphemously, did they suffer? At the hands of poverty, war, brutality, violence, and loneliness? They cared for others—or tried—until their dying day. They were silenced, often afraid. Some, like my Oma, were prone to rages, striking out at whoever they had power over, usually a child in their household. They overproduced the misery and sadness they had inherited. They were stuck, drained by and for others, their resources depleted.

I have not returned to life for that. I choose a different burden, not to be the carrier of others' demons—a new path. And I come back needing a new name, one that doesn't hold the suffering of all my women ancestors. I think about names—my first one, my middle one, my last one, my mother's names—until it hits me: I already have a new name. I was given one before I got sick, the one I received as my son's mother. *Mina*. The name he gifted to me. His birth also gave birth.

Mina. A nod to the Slavic word *maminka* used throughout the continent for mom. Mina: the creation stems from a frequent practice in queer communities to find a new term when a child has two mothers. Sometimes, like in my case, the non-birth mother elects something other than the traditional "mom." Mina: an intimate word between my son and me, and one that my friends parrot sometimes because he uses it so much, often in rapid succession when he is calling me. Mina: the first word I remember his little mouth forming. I can picture it even now.

Mina is also the name in Francis Ford Coppola's film adaptation of Dracula's reincarnated bride. He finds her again through ages and centuries, weeping as he sees her face, human and pulsing with life. Mina survives his death, mortal in the face of his predatory and violent immortality. She emerges from the chamber where she has destroyed him, sobbing, covered in his blood.

Mina, a name to begin again, was chosen for me, by me. The name used by the person who calls my name more than any other—in the middle of the night, when he is scared, when he is annoyed, when he wants attention. Last night, I heard him from the hall, singing in the bathtub: *Mina, miiiiina, mina, mina.*

We share the name as he and I shared the experience of cancer. The time in which he faces inwardly toward me is nearing an end. He is just at that age, older now. He is ready to turn outward and start exploring the world. In *The Creative Spirit,* June Jordan said that children are how the world begins again and again. But, for me, his early years will always be marked both by his beginnings and the beginning of my cancer. The years he has been alive have been the hardest of my life, hard in a way that you realize nothing before them was truly hard. Just as he learned the name of plants and animals, he gathered that I might die. It is almost too much for me to absorb. We both will live with the memories of him clinging to my hot, bald, silent, drugged body. He was angry then, with too limited a vocabulary to name this fact. When I ask experts how to help him with all this history when he gets older, they tell me the one thing I do not want to hear. Keep talking about it with him, they say, don't pretend it didn't happen. I pray Mina will be up to the task. To do this for him, I have to do it for myself. I have to keep talking about it, I have to keep remembering.

●●●

It was easier for me to chronicle the sickness when it was acute. The healing is much more awkward, lurching around in the pools and mud of my habits. I could let go of outcomes when I was facing my own death, but, with the body and mind's return to higher functioning, the urge to take control rears its ugly head again. My insomnia returns, my churning grievances, my deep fears of loss—a different loss than I feared in the idea of relinquishing my own life.

Not all cancer patients get better, even if our bodies seem to function again, even if our hair grows back and our eyelashes reappear and our eyes clear out of the starstruck shine they have during chemo. Many of us were not well to start with: overproduction and excess consumed and overran us before our cells joined in.

Of the few friends my age who have been dealing with cancer, I am the only one who doesn't worry about it returning every morning I wake up. Suspiciously, however, I go through bouts of fearfulness about other things. Mostly my kid, his well-being, my family, etc.

Before the pandemic, it might have been run-of-the-mill for the final section of a book such as this to conclude with a strident feminist call to action about the lack of funding for cancer research—particularly ovarian cancer, which ravages poor people, LGBTQ people, Jewish people, and anyone with ovaries who is too marginalized, poverty-stricken, or exhausted to see a doctor.

Here, towards the end, one might talk about the mental illnesses common for those dealing with ovarian cancer and its aftermath: depression, anxiety, adjustment disorder, and others. But depression and anxiety are washing over our whole society. In certain respects, the traumas suffered by cancer survivors are mirrored throughout our culture. So many of us are just holding on, just existing.

It may be that drawing strict divisions between the ravages we suffer isn't helpful. At this point in my life, I try very hard to visualize and meditate on the things that connect me to others, not only the ways I am set apart. Still, maladies are not warm and fuzzy things to have in common with others. Sterilization is not something I romanticize as a shared condition. My nephew tells me that, in his experience working in insurance, companies are quick to pay for sterilization but rarely want to cover the costs for ovarian or cervical cancer care, let alone fertility and family-making costs for those of us who are queer, sterilized, or both.

That does feel like a decent soapbox to get up on, I would say. We live in a country where a small and potent minority is obsessed with forcing women—and anyone who can get pregnant—to have babies they do not want. Even if we are deeply traumatized or die in the process. This same powerful faction will do a great deal to make sure that people like me (queer, sterilized, cancer patients, solo parents, and moms) have a tough time having more babies. They will do even more to make sure that people they hate even more than me (poor, queer people of color, people with disabilities) find it next to impossible to have babies.

They want us to give up. Just like they want so many people to give up, they want us to give up on being mothers. They want us to give up on parenting in our way. They want us to give up on building the families and spheres of nurturance we want. They want us to give up because they don't want the children we raise to inherit the world. They don't want the babies we raise (many of whom will be powerful, resilient, sensitive, visionary, and living deeply in the now) to reach adulthood intact and healthy. They don't want my son to have the family he has, in all its complexity and all its pain. They don't want me to have another child.

Progressives used to say that those in power are afraid of us. I don't know if that is true. What I do know is that there is a small, greedy, delusional, violent part of this society that wants to dominate and confine the rest of us.

I push past them and through them and their twisted will to dominate and subdue us. I push past them and through them in my mothering dreams because I know that my children can know the strength given to me through my proximity to death, what I survived, and the life that grew out of that.

As a white woman, I never fully connected with Audre Lorde's idea that we are powerful because we have survived. I simply had not survived enough until this point in my life. I didn't know shit about that. Not really. I chuckle at how little I still understand that statement. But now I know some power in my survival. I alone know what precisely I survived. Cancer is such a lonely journey in so many ways; I think one survives it in large part to the degree one is *not* left alone. We have a much better chance of surviving it when we are in community, messy, contradictory, raw-ass community. But we experience its actual impact on our bodies alone. Every time I see a bald head with an eyebrowless face in public, I marvel at how the person radiates a solitary pain, atomized, cut apart from others.

I choose each day to improve my mind, to work to match my powerful and fragile body and its slow, steady healing. This is so hard and often bloody. I must cut through the veins and tentacles that connect me to old patterns, old ways of being, and my old addictions to sorrow and nostalgia. Wherever I cut, the wound bleeds, and I feel exposed, judged for making the gash, for asserting a boundary. I watch the nectarines in my large kitchen bowl thinking about healing and boundaries: watch them before they are ripe, ripe, and just past.

Doctors tell me that even in remission, ovarian cancer patients often experience weakness, fatigue, neuropathy, depression, anxiety, fear of recurrence, and sleep problems. On top of that, surviving ovarian cancer leaves me at higher risk for other cancers, cancers that really scare me. I consider daily how to meet this information, and how to engage it. It does not consume me and, in some ways, it helps me remember I don't have to produce at the speed I did before.

I never sleep through the night unmedicated. But neither do most of the women in my family. I am often weary, my joints sore, and yet I also relish the fact that I can still go for a run on a cool morning, or drink three glasses of champagne if I want to.

The lessons of cancer, like those of parenting, have a lot to teach all of us these days. It has taught me a great deal.

I can still do things when I am tired. I can function on sleep that is broken. I must take naps and rest. I must be still and then in motion again—and then still again. Sometimes people around me try to gently discourage me from my post-cancer dreams and plans. They worry I may be too tired for more children, for my work, and for the responsibilities that I choose to take on. But my fatigue is manageable, and easily treated with more downtime and sufficient time alone. Being tired, I have learned, does not mean you have to give up. It does mean I have to do things differently. I must ask for things—loved ones to watch my child for an hour so I can write or just lie down in my car with music on for a few minutes. I must ask for money, more money, I must accept that the monthly bills are what they are. What I do have is peace of mind—lonely and quiet peace sometimes, but peace of mind nonetheless.

The monsoon season in Arizona begins giving way to desert autumn, little by little. When you move more slowly, there are more opportunities to see the sky, watch the air change. Everything green in Phoenix, truly bright, electric green, is being cared for by someone. Sure, I get it: we use a lot of water on plants that don't grow here naturally. But I also try to see the other side, the caring side. My plants shine green in the windows of my house.

According to Alice Walker, everything we love can be saved. I don't agree. Or maybe I don't agree anymore. Times have changed. We live at the end of an era, the end of a mode and way of doing and being. Creatures who live in such a time don't get to decide what can be saved. We can only play our part, pushing in a direction we can live with. Baba Yaga stands over us. Sacrifice is not meaningless, but most sacrifices involve more time and loss than we could possibly imagine. *Silly Children,* Baba Yaga says, *most of you don't even know what the word means. It is not giving something up. It means letting something die, so that something else can live. That is what making a sacrifice is.*

Healing means feeling raw again, feeling the proximity to my own shame, grief, awkwardness, history, and reactivity. In truth, I was a reactor for much of my life. Proactivity is scary—taking responsibility for my life instead of just responding. Finding the truth inside what I want and acting on it is frightening. Perhaps, that is why this book scares me.

The journey back to life prompts one question: what can the creator not do? She has been with us from the beginning and she awaits us beyond the end. She took pecans, dates, kale, strawberries, and some amount of sleep and turned them into a new face for me: complete with eyebrows and eyelashes, and eyes that cry non-toxic tears. She made a half-alive being—part dolphin, part amphibian—back into a human woman. She healed what was broken, in such an incredibly short time. She is beyond myth, legend, or sacred text. I will never cease to wonder why so many people must look further than her to find a God. You walk upon her; she gave the sac and the canal that birthed you; she gives you air to breathe. Yet, we make her into our own image. She will never be in our image, so far beyond us is her design, her love poured out onto this earth and into our bodies.

But get yourself someone, another human, who loves you when you become a slick and hairless other and then must find your way back to being a woman. Find yourself a woman who loves you through that: she will know not only what love is, but who God is. She will know her true name.

CHAPTER 11

Barn's Burnt Down, Autumn 2022

August 31, 2022

On this day, a year ago, I finished chemotherapy. The last day of August last year was one of the most painful of my life. Out of my six journeys to the chemo underworld, the last was the worst. By coincidence or design beyond my understanding, I happen to have to go to Mayo Clinic on the same day, this year. I drive myself there. The fortress in the desert feels familiar and unfamiliar. A year ago I saw tigers and a bright green jungle in my Benadryl dreams in the chair. I remember seeing the mountains, high and bright over the desert, from the window in my chemo cubicle.

I walk inside and notice the emergency stretcher in the corner, packed with equipment, ready to go. During one of my earlier visits, a chemo-ward nurse nonchalantly told my best friend how some patients with COVID had coded in their chemo recliners. No one had known they had COVID, so it is important for patients to take COVID tests before each infusion. I remember my best friend's stricken face. The nurse had noticed and then told her not to worry: all three times it had happened the patients' hearts had started beating again. I heard the story but was high as a kite, and thought, *how interesting COVID interacts with chemo poison that way, the crossing of streams of plague and poison.* I consider the stretcher in the corner again. How many cancer patients died on it, and how quickly were their deaths forgotten?

I enter the heart of the fortress to see my doctor, a surgeon with the personality of a precise knife. She gives me an anal and vaginal exam, the skin she touches feels thin, and she lets me know it will only feel thinner, more fragile, and brittle as I age if they don't give me moisturizers and creams. She and the nurse remind themselves how young I am, how unusual that is. This reminds me of that fact, as well. After I leave the examination room, I go to the bathroom and cry my eyes out. I wipe my face and look in the mirror. My eyes are hazel when I cry—the color of my sister's. I think about my mom's bright blue eyes, then about how strong she is, how angry she had to be to find that strength. I look up to her greatly at this point in my life. I have finally learned how lucky I am to have her spirit, her fire, her force inside of me. I make a prayer for her. How much her strength must have cost her—always being the strong tree that so many others sat beneath or hid behind. I say a prayer for my father as well, grateful for how he showed me that a strong woman with strong boundaries can be loved and adored by someone as strong and hopeful as himself.

I have always hated Shel Silverstein's book *The Giving Tree.* The tree gives to the little boy over and over, bit by bit by bit until she disappears. I do not want to give myself away, limb by limb. I do not want to be drained, a vial of blood at a time. I am not a stone on the shore, where each wave wears me down a little more. I plan to walk away from the waves.

I leave the bathroom and make my way out of the maze of hallways. I go to the lab and, despite what I'd just promised myself, get vial after vial of blood drawn. The phlebotomist notes that my veins are "shot." I tell her I should have gotten a port during chemotherapy. She points out that I would have had a scar on my chest. I would have taken that happily, I tell her, to spare my veins. According to her, no regular nurse should draw blood from me now, only a phlebotomist. She, like all medical professionals, says chemo in my arm that whole time was a huge mistake. I tell her I fell into the gap that was COVID and care. She nods.

I drive home with a bandage on my arm. I think about how much of this story, the story of my cancer, is omitted to protect the privacy of others. Perhaps that is often true of a writer's life. This is the first time I felt entitled to write a book, and it took cancer. So, I would only newly know. The women who held up my world while I was sick will not be seen here, at least not seen with a wide aperture that lets all their light in. Not in the ways that, perhaps, they should be seen. I could never portray their part in these events accurately. I can only tell my story. Suffice it to say, it is incredibly rare that I must drive myself home. I have rarely come to the Mayo fortress alone.

I go to the grocery store with the goal to spend less than forty dollars. It is only 11 a.m. but it is already 105 degrees. I buy primarily living foods, or recently alive foods—spinach, broccoli, red pepper, nectarines, and strawberries. Cancer left me reluctantly vegan, though not a strict one at all. In fact, the night before I ate at McDonald's. But when I go to grocery stores, I feel the urge to buy foods that look whole and lively. It has become a compulsion since chemotherapy. I no longer really enjoy mammal flesh, though beings that swam in the sea are still mostly appealing. The cashier looks at my bandaged arm strangely. I spend $39.45 and have a challenging time carrying my bags to the car by myself because my left arm aches, the veins burning inside of it.

This is a year out. This is a woman in remission. This is a young woman whose life was saved and still it hurts.

What must those who are "a year out" feel if they are sixty? Seventy? Truly alone?

I have returned again to stubbornly recording my every emotion as if I was a scientific experiment—but a feminist one. I am documenting all the moments today, a year out. I do so for all the women who can't. Many of them are dead, some almost completely forgotten.

I was filled with rage last weekend when I read a *New York Times* list of the best fifty memoirs of all time because so many of them were famous white men talking about their glory days in certain boroughs of New York City. In a huge world, filled with people and places, why are the stories of value so specific and narrow? I imagine all the women, of all ages and races, who enter the Mayo Clinic alone, who check themselves in for their appointments, who hobble back out to their cars alone.

Who has the ego to write a memoir? Who believes our days are worth chronicling? Who reads and cares about which stories?

What do those memoir-writing men know about life, real life, the raw life that Baba Yaga governs? I do not care about their stories. I do not care because of who I am, what I have seen, and what I have been through. I do not care because these are not the stories we need right now. We need real stories, not pissing contests.

In the story I have shared with you, I am not who I set out to be, not who I wanted to be. In the car, from the grocery store, with my burning skin and aching arm, I think of the old, Indigenous lesbian of Canada, Ferron. In a recent interview, she was asked what she wished for. She said she wanted to die Indigenous and a lesbian, a wish she knew she would get. I think of how she always said that when love finally calls you don't wilt upon its stage.

I am a writer, usually so literal, but the truths of our age are riddles for those who care to puzzle them out. Our enduring ancestors, those who never gave up on us and never will, sing not in unison but in an uncomfortable chorus. They will be with us until the end and on the other side of it.

Months ago, I thought I knew how this story ended. I thought it was with my Solstice dream, my son and I under the great evergreen tree. I thought it ended poetically; I thought it ended in the spirit realm. But the spirit realm is the domain of those who currently do not reside in bodies. I am firmly in mine. I have learned a new definition of the word "grounded"—a word that many hold up as an ideal of how to move in the world. But, just like healing, being grounded does not always feel pleasant. To be so deep inside my body, to feel so much. Many days I want to run screaming from the experience. All the drama, all the self-torment, all the living without boundaries I see around me; I sometimes feel jealous of the physical ability that people must have to pull it off. I have so little. A blessing? That is the question.

Some of us caught up in mothering are consumed and want to be consumed, to see every tiny, practical thing be reborn, as new as when children see them for the first time. The world becomes small, domestic, and, at least in my experience, bright and glorious. Some of us love giving in the way that mothering requires, and some of us burn in shame because we do not want to give that much.

This book forced itself from me. It bubbled up through the pavement of the Mayo fortress, up through sickness and drug use, and made itself seen and heard even when I wanted to give it no time, when I wanted only to be well again, to mother and work and love.

After my son was born, I knew deep down I was lost in my personal life, and a tree in Prescott, Arizona, told me as I lay under her that none of my worries mattered because, when I became a mother, I became a warrior. I think this book warriored itself through me, marched through and out of me like an army of dead women. I am a year out from cancer, and most parts of me are well. The bright purple soup of Poland healed something that still hurt deep within me. I healed. I felt alive. I felt the living around me.

As for me, I am here on purpose and the purpose isn't always fun. I am a force. I am a boundary. I am a conduit. I am willing to save myself in this time, even if others will not save themselves. I am willing to protect myself: the warm creature I fought so hard to keep alive. I am a skin-shedder. I am glistening, vulnerable, bright, and new. I am needed at this time. I will find the many others also ready for now, and we will lead.

I never wanted to be what I am now: a story where the bridge behind you has burned. There is no way for me but forward, there is nowhere to hide. This is etched into my body: and this is the only body I have. The options I once indulged in are gone. I will stay this way, be this way. I end where I began—All In—not always by choice. All in with fate, not faith; all in with the pattern of all life, not beliefs. Barn's burnt down, now I see the moon. A moon so bright, it is as though the barn was never there at all.